Fiona Mapp

Success

AQA
GCSE Mathematics
Foundation
Workbook

Contents

- 4 Homework diary
- 5 Revision & exam tips

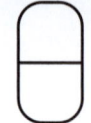

Statistics and probability

- 6 Collecting data
- 8 Representing data
- 10 Scatter graphs & correlation
- 12 Averages 1
- 14 Averages 2
- 16 Probability 1
- 18 Probability 2

Revised

Number

- 20 Number revision
- 22 Numbers
- 24 Positive & negative numbers
- 26 Working with numbers
- 28 Fractions
- 30 Decimals
- 32 Percentages 1
- 34 Percentages 2
- 36 Fractions, decimals & percentages
- 38 Approximating & using a calculator
- 40 Ratio
- 42 Indices

Revised

Algebra

Revised

- 44 Algebra
- 46 Formulae
- 48 Equations 1
- 50 Equations 2 & inequalities
- 52 Number patterns & sequences
- 54 Straight-line graphs
- 56 Quadratic graphs
- 58 Interpreting graphs

Geometry and measures

Revised

- 60 Shapes
- 62 Solids
- 64 Angles
- 66 Bearings & scale drawings
- 68 Transformations 1
- 70 Transformations 2
- 72 Symmetry & constructions
- 74 Loci & coordinates
- 76 Measures & measurement 1
- 78 Measures & measurement 2
- 80 Pythagoras' theorem
- 82 Area of 2D shapes
- 84 Volume of 3D shapes

- 86 Mixed GCSE-style questions
- 94 Answers to mixed GCSE-style questions

Homework diary

TOPIC	SCORE
Collecting data	/20
Representing data	/24
Scatter graphs & correlation	/22
Averages 1	/30
Averages 2	/23
Probability 1	/30
Probability 2	/22
Number revision	/27
Numbers	/42
Positive & negative numbers	/29
Working with numbers	/38
Fractions	/49
Decimals	/36
Percentages 1	/36
Percentages 2	/38
Fractions, decimals & percentages	/25
Approximating & using a calculator	/34
Ratio	/32
Indices	/53
Algebra	/36
Formulae	/31
Equations 1	/49
Equations 2 & inequalities	/29
Number patterns & sequences	/29
Straight-line graphs	/23
Quadratic graphs	/20
Interpreting graphs	/15
Shapes	/24
Solids	/21
Angles	/34
Bearings & scale drawings	/20
Transformations 1	/22
Transformations 2	/19
Symmetry & constructions	/21
Loci & coordinates	/15
Measures & measurement 1	/22
Measures & measurement 2	/36
Pythagoras' theorem	/31
Area of 2D shapes	/30
Volume of 3D shapes	/32

Revision & exam tips

Planning and revising:
- Mathematics should be revised **actively.** You should be doing **more than just reading**.
- Find out the dates of your first mathematics examination. Make an examination and revision timetable.
- After completing a topic in school, go through the topic again in the **GCSE Success Revision Guide**. Copy out the **main points**, **results** and **formulae** into a notebook or use a **highlighter** to emphasise them.
- Try to write out the **key points** from **memory**. Check what you have written and see if there are any differences.
- Revise in short bursts of about **30 minutes**, followed by a **short break**.
- Learn **facts** from your exercise books, notebooks and the **Success Revision Guide**. **Memorise** any formula you need to learn.
- Learn with a friend to make it easier and more fun!
- Do the **multiple-choice** and **short-answer** questions in this book and check your answers to see how much you know.
- Once you feel **confident** that you know the topic, do the **GCSE-style** questions in this book. **Highlight** the key words in the question, **plan** your answer and then go back and **check** that you have answered the question.
- **Make a note** of any topics that you do not understand and **go back through** the notes again.

Different types of questions:
- On the **GCSE Mathematics papers** you will have several types of questions:
  Calculate – In these questions you need to work out the answer. Remember that it is important to show full working out.
  Explain – These questions want you to explain, with a mathematical reason or calculation, what the answer is.
  Show – These questions usually require you to show, with mathematical justification, what the answer is.
  Write down or state – These questions require no explanation or working out.
  Prove – These questions want you to set out a concise logical argument, making the reasons clear.
  Deduce – These questions make use of an earlier answer to establish a result.

On the day:
- **Follow the instructions** on the exam paper. Make sure that you understand what any **symbols** mean.
- Make sure that you **read the question** carefully so that you give the answer that an examiner wants.
- Always **show your working**; you may pick up some marks even if your final answer is wrong.
- Do **rough calculations** to check your answers and make sure that they are **reasonable**.
- When carrying out a calculation, **do not round the answer until the end**, otherwise your final answer will not be as accurate as is needed.
- Lay out your working **carefully** and **concisely**. Write down the calculations that you are going to make. You usually get marks for showing a **correct method**.
- Make your drawings and graphs **neat** and **accurate**.
- Know what is on the **formula sheet** and make sure that you **learn** those formulae that are not on it.
- If you cannot do a question, **leave it out** and **go back** to it at the end.
- Keep an eye on the time. Allow enough time to check through your answers.
- If you finish early, check through everything very carefully and try to fill in any gaps.
- Try to write something even if you are not sure about it. Leaving an empty space will score you no marks.

Good luck!

Collecting data

Multiple-choice questions

Choose just one answer, a, b, c or d. Circle your choice.

1) What is the name given to data you collect yourself?
   a) Continuous   b) Primary   c) Secondary   d) Discrete   (1 mark)

2) What type of data is usually obtained by counting?
   a) Continuous   b) Primary   c) Secondary   d) Discrete   (1 mark)

3) What is the name given to data in which values merge from one category to the next?
   a) Continuous   b) Primary   c) Secondary   d) Discrete   (1 mark)

4) What type of data gives a word as an answer?
   a) Quantitative   b) Qualitative   c) Continuous   d) Discrete   (1 mark)

Score / 4

Short-answer questions

Answer all parts of each question.

1) Hannah and Thomas are collecting some data on the types of books read by students. Draw a suitable data collection sheet for this information.

(3 marks)

2) Imran and Annabelle are designing a survey to use in school. One of their questions is: 'How much time do you spend doing homework per night?'

0–1 hr	1–2 hrs	2–3 hrs	3–4 hrs

What is wrong with this question? Rewrite the question to improve it.

(2 marks)

3) Emily decides to carry out a survey on how much football people watch on television. She decides to ask 50 men outside a football ground on Saturday afternoon. Explain why her results will be biased.

(2 marks)

Score / 7

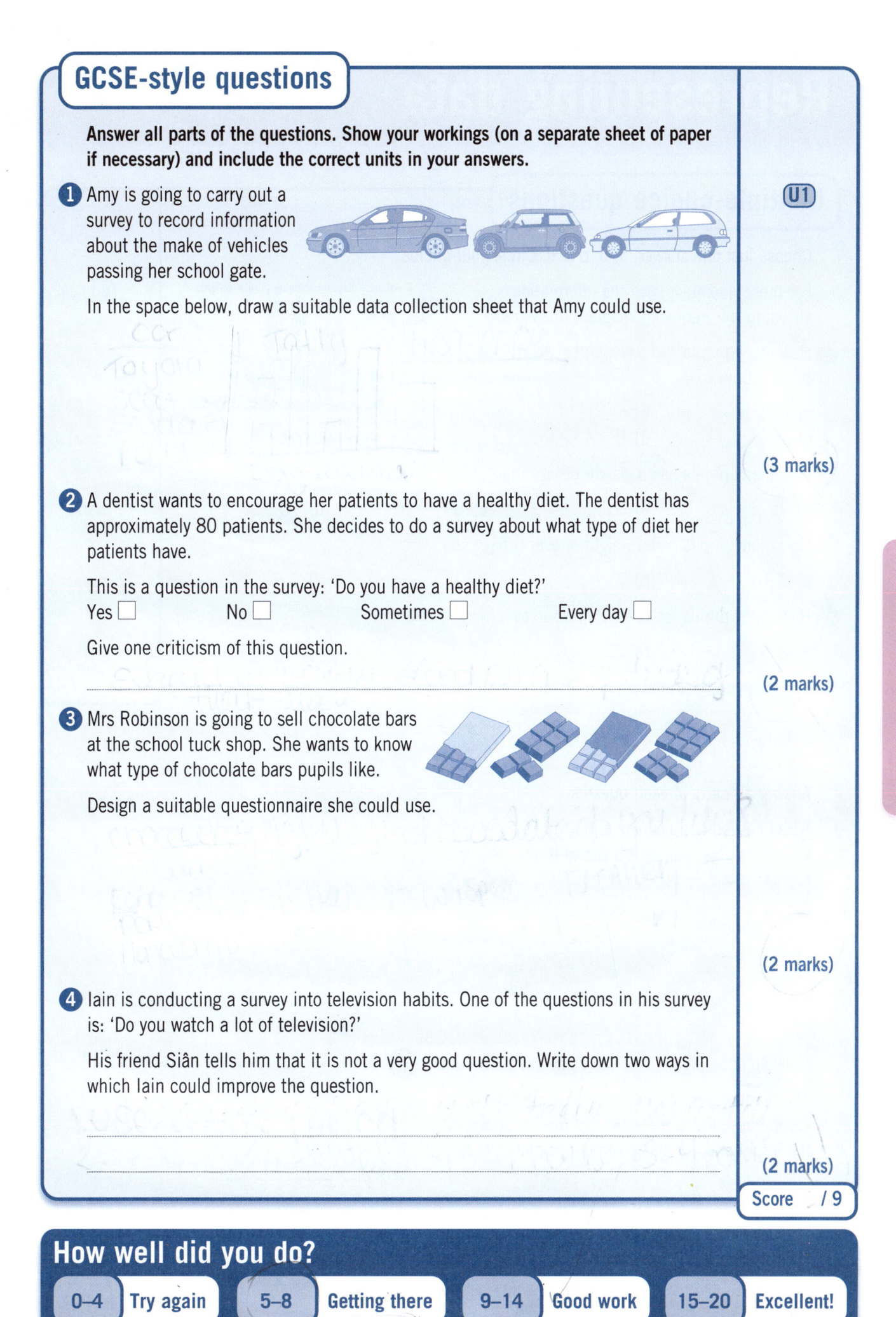

GCSE-style questions

Answer all parts of the questions. Show your workings (on a separate sheet of paper if necessary) and include the correct units in your answers.

1 Amy is going to carry out a survey to record information about the make of vehicles passing her school gate.

In the space below, draw a suitable data collection sheet that Amy could use.

(U1)

(3 marks)

2 A dentist wants to encourage her patients to have a healthy diet. The dentist has approximately 80 patients. She decides to do a survey about what type of diet her patients have.

This is a question in the survey: 'Do you have a healthy diet?'
Yes ☐   No ☐   Sometimes ☐   Every day ☐

Give one criticism of this question.

(2 marks)

3 Mrs Robinson is going to sell chocolate bars at the school tuck shop. She wants to know what type of chocolate bars pupils like.

Design a suitable questionnaire she could use.

(2 marks)

4 Iain is conducting a survey into television habits. One of the questions in his survey is: 'Do you watch a lot of television?'

His friend Siân tells him that it is not a very good question. Write down two ways in which Iain could improve the question.

(2 marks)

Score   / 9

How well did you do?

0–4 Try again   5–8 Getting there   9–14 Good work   15–20 Excellent!

For more information on this topic, see pages 4–5 of your Success Revision Guide.

Representing data

Multiple-choice questions

Choose just one answer, a, b, c or d. Circle your choice.

For these questions, use the information shown in the frequency diagram (histogram).

1 How many pupils had a weight between 50 and 55kg?

a) 4   b) 6
c) 10   d) 8

(1 mark)

2 How many pupils had a weight of less than 50kg?

a) 7   b) 8   c) 9   d) 10

(1 mark)

3 How many pupils had a weight of over 60kg?

a) 1   b) 2   c) 3   d) 4

(1 mark)

4 How many pupils took part in the survey?

a) 8   b) 22   c) 5   d) 20

(1 mark)

Score / 4

Short-answer questions

Answer all parts of each question.

1 Sarah carried out a survey to find the favourite flavours of crisps of students in her year group. Her results are shown in the table below.

Crisp flavour	Number of students
Cheese and onion	21
Salt and vinegar	30
Beef	18
Smoky bacon	3

Draw an accurate pie chart to show this information.

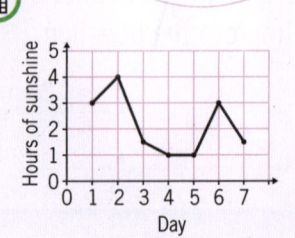

(4 marks)

2 The number of hours of sunshine during the first seven days in May are shown on the line graph. Use the information on the graph to complete the table.

Day	1	2	3	4	5	6	7
Hours of sunshine	3		1.5	1	1		

(3 marks)

Score / 7

GCSE-style questions

Answer all parts of the questions. Show your workings (on a separate sheet of paper if necessary) and include the correct units in your answers.

1 The pictogram shows the number of DVDs borrowed from a shop on a Friday and Saturday.

Friday	● ● ● ◖
Saturday	● ● ● ● ◢
Sunday	
Monday	

Key: ● = 4 DVDs

a) Write down the number of DVDs borrowed on…

   i) Friday .... (1 mark)

   ii) Saturday. .... (1 mark)

b) On Sunday, 13 DVDs were borrowed. On Monday, 6 DVDs were borrowed. Show this information on the pictogram. (2 marks)

2 Jackie works in a newsagents. One week she collects some data on the flavour of crisps her customers bought. Jackie makes a bar chart of her results.

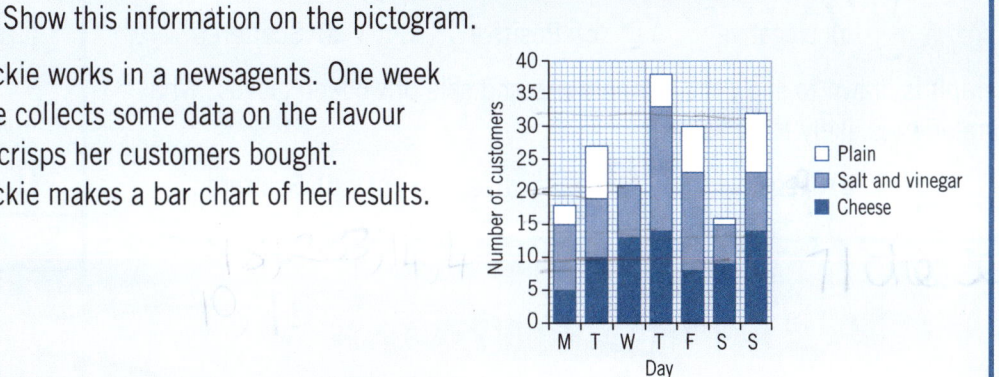

a) On which day was the highest number of packets of crisps sold? .... (1 mark)

b) On which day were no plain flavour crisps sold? .... (1 mark)

c) How many packets of crisps were sold on Sunday? .... (1 mark)

d) Jackie says that she sells more cheese-flavour crisps. Decide whether Jackie is right, giving a reason for your answer.

.... (3 marks)

3 The table shows the heights of children in a class.

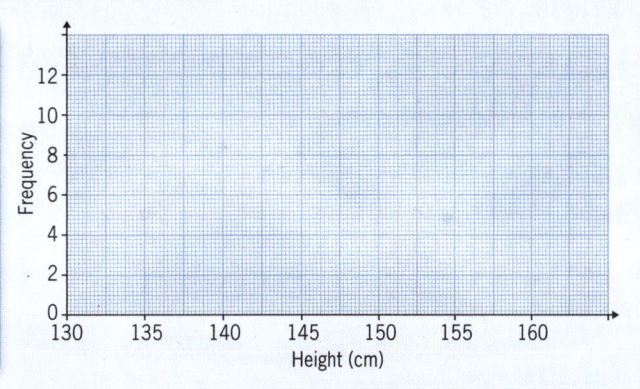

Height h (in cm)	Frequency
$130 \leq h < 135$	5
$135 \leq h < 140$	9
$140 \leq h < 145$	7
$145 \leq h < 150$	4
$150 \leq h < 155$	5
$155 \leq h < 160$	2

Draw a frequency polygon for this data on the grid provided. (3 marks)

Score / 13

How well did you do?

0–4 Try again   5–9 Getting there   10–16 Good work   17–24 Excellent!

For more information on this topic, see pages 6–9 of your Success Revision Guide.

Scatter graphs & correlation

Multiple-choice questions

Choose just one answer, a, b, c or d. Circle your choice.

1 A scatter graph is drawn to show the height and weight of some students. What type of correlation is likely to be shown?

   a) Zero   b) Negative   c) Positive   d) Scattered   (1 mark)

2 A scatter graph is drawn to show the maths scores and waist measurements of a group of students. What type of correlation is likely to be shown?

   a) Zero   b) Negative   c) Positive   d) Scattered   (1 mark)

3 A scatter graph is drawn to show the temperature and sale of woollen gloves. What type of correlation is likely to be shown?

   a) Zero   b) Negative   c) Positive   d) Scattered   (1 mark)

U1

Score /3

Short-answer questions

Answer all parts of each question.

1 Some statements have been written on cards:

   Positive correlation   Negative correlation   No correlation

Decide which card best describes these relationships.

   a) The outside temperature and the sales of ice lollies   (1 mark)

   b) The number of glasses of juice poured and the amount of juice left in the jug   (1 mark)

   c) The mass of a person and his/her waist measurement   (1 mark)

   d) The height of a person and his/her IQ   (1 mark)

2 The scatter graph shows the marks scored in mathematics and physics examinations.

   a) Describe the relationship between the mathematics and physics scores.

       _____   (1 mark)

   b) Draw a line of best fit on the scatter graph.   (1 mark)

   c) Use your line of best fit to estimate the mathematics score that Jonathan is likely to obtain if he has a physics score of 75%.

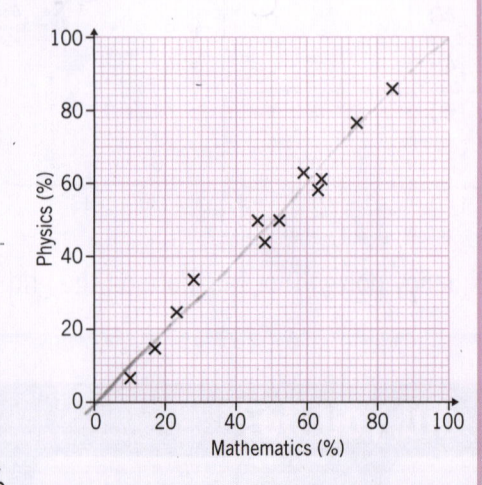

       _____ %   (1 mark)

Score /7

GCSE-style questions

Answer all parts of the questions. Show your workings (on a separate sheet of paper if necessary) and include the correct units in your answers.

1 The table shows the ages of some children and the total number of hours of sleep they had between noon on Saturday and noon on Sunday.

Age (years)	2	6	5	3	12	9	2	10	5	10	7	11	12	3
No. of hours of sleep	15	13.1	13.2	14.8	10.1	11.8	15.6	11.6	13.5	11.8	12.8	10.2	9.5	14

a) Plot the information from the table in the form of a scatter graph.

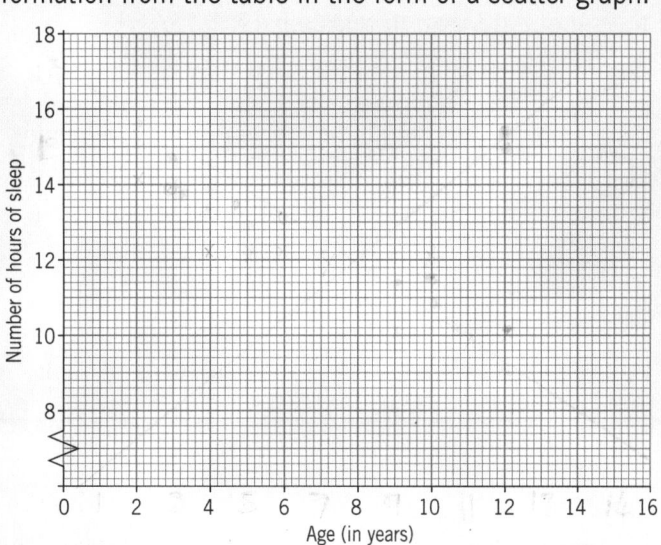

(4 marks)

b) Describe the correlation between the age of the children in years and the total number of hours of sleep they had.

(2 marks)

c) Draw a line of best fit on your scatter graph.

(1 mark)

d) Estimate the total number of hours of sleep for a 4-year-old child.

(2 marks)

e) Explain why the line of best fit only gives an estimate for the number of hours slept.

(2 marks)

f) A child psychologist states, '5-year-old children have between 15 and 16 hours of sleep a night.' Decide, based on the data above, whether the child psychologist is correct.

(1 mark)

Score   / 12

How well did you do?

0–5 Try again   6–11 Getting there   12–16 Good work   17–22 Excellent!

For more information on this topic, see pages 10–11 of your Success Revision Guide.

Averages 1

Multiple-choice questions

Choose just one answer, a, b, c or d. Circle your choice.

1) What is the mean of this set of data? 2, 7, 1, 4, 2, 6, 2, 5, 2, 6
   a) 4.2   b) 3.6   c) 3.7   d) 3.9   (1 mark)

2) What is the median value of the set of data used in question 1?
   a) 2   b) 3   c) 4   d) 5   (1 mark)

3) A dice is thrown and the scores are noted. The results are shown in the table below. What is the mean dice score?

Dice score	1	2	3	4	5	6
Frequency	12	15	10	8	14	13

   a) 5   b) 3   c) 4   d) 3.5   (1 mark)

Score / 3

Short-answer questions

Answer all parts of each question.

1) Here are some number cards:

   8 7 11 4 2 1 3 12 4 4

   State whether the following statements, which refer to the number cards above, are **true** or **false**.

   a) The range of the number cards is 1–11 .... (1 mark)
   b) The mean of the number cards is 5.6 .... (1 mark)
   c) The median of the number cards is 5 .... (1 mark)
   d) The mode of the number cards is 4 .... (1 mark)

2) A baked beans factory claims, 'On average, a tin of baked beans contains 141 beans.'
   In order to check the accuracy of this claim, a sample of 20 tins was taken and the number of beans in each tin counted.

Number of beans	137	138	139	140	141	142	143	144
Number of tins	1	1	1	2	5	4	4	2

   a) Calculate the mean number of beans per tin. .... (1 mark)
   b) Explain briefly whether you think the manufacturer is justified in making its claim.
   .... (1 mark)

3) The mean of 7, 9, 10, 18, x and 17 is 13. What is the value of x? .... (2 marks)

Score / 8

GCSE-style questions

Answer all parts of the questions. Show your workings (on a separate sheet of paper if necessary) and include the correct units in your answers.

1 Grace made a list of the ages of some children in her swimming club.

7, 8, 7, 14, 10, 12, 12, 7, 12, 12, 11, 15

   a) Find the median age of the children. .... (2 marks)

   b) Find the range of the ages of the children. .... (1 mark)

   c) Find the mean age of the children, correct to 1 decimal place.

.... (3 marks)

2 Here are three hidden cards:

[?] [?] [?]

The mode of the three numbers is 7. The mean of the three numbers is 9. What are the three numbers?

.... (3 marks)

3 Some students took a test. The table gives information about their marks in the test.

Mark	Frequency
3	2
4	5
5	11
6	2

Work out the mean mark.

.... (3 marks)

4 Simon has sat three examinations. His mean score is 65. To pass the unit, he needs to get an average of 69. What score must he get in the fourth and final examination to pass the unit?

.... (3 marks)

5 A company employs three women and seven men. The mean weekly wage of the ten employees is £464. The mean weekly wage of the three women is £520. Calculate the mean weekly wage of the seven men.

£..

.... (4 marks)

Score / 19

How well did you do?

0–6 Try again   7–12 Getting there   13–22 Good work   23–30 Excellent!

For more information on this topic, see pages 12–13 of your Success Revision Guide.

Averages 2

Multiple-choice questions

Choose just one answer, a, b, c or d. Circle your choice.

The following questions are based on the information given in the table opposite about the time taken in seconds to swim 50 metres.

Time (t seconds)	Frequency (f)
$0 \leqslant t < 30$	1
$30 \leqslant t < 60$	2
$60 \leqslant t < 90$	4
$90 \leqslant t < 120$	6
$120 \leqslant t < 150$	7
$150 \leqslant t < 180$	2

1 How many people swam 50 metres in less than 60 seconds?

a) 2   b) 4
c) 3   d) 6

(1 mark)

2 Which of the intervals is the modal class?

a) $60 \leqslant t < 90$ b) $120 \leqslant t < 150$ c) $30 \leqslant t < 60$ d) $90 \leqslant t < 120$

(1 mark)

3 Which of the class intervals contains the median value?

a) $90 \leqslant t < 120$ b) $150 \leqslant t < 180$ c) $120 \leqslant t < 150$ d) $60 \leqslant t < 90$

(1 mark)

4 What is an estimate for the mean time taken to swim 50 metres?

a) 105 seconds   b) 385 seconds   c) 100 seconds   d) 125 seconds

(1 mark)

Score / 4

Short-answer questions

Answer all parts of each question.

1 The length of some seedlings is shown in the table opposite.

Calculate an estimate for the mean length of the seedlings.

Length L (mm)	Number of seedlings
$0 \leqslant L < 10$	3
$10 \leqslant L < 20$	5
$20 \leqslant L < 30$	9
$30 \leqslant L < 40$	2
$40 \leqslant L < 50$	1

Mean = _____ mm

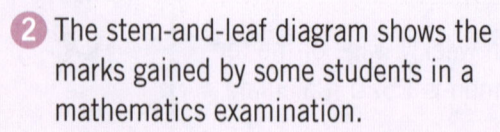

(4 marks)

2 The stem-and-leaf diagram shows the marks gained by some students in a mathematics examination.

```
1 | 2 5 7
2 | 6 9
3 | 4 5 5 7
4 | 2 7 7 7 7
5 | 2
```
Key: 1 | 2 = 12 marks

Using the stem-and-leaf diagram, work out…

a) the mode _____ (1 mark)

b) the median _____ (1 mark)

c) the range. _____ (1 mark)

Score / 7

GCSE-style questions

Answer all parts of the questions. Show your workings (on a separate sheet of paper if necessary) and include the correct units in your answers.

1 A psychologist records the times, to the nearest minute, taken by 20 students to complete a logic problem. Here are the results.

| 12 | 22 | 31 | 36 | 35 | 14 | 27 | 23 | 19 | 25 |
| 15 | 17 | 15 | 27 | 32 | 38 | 41 | 18 | 27 | 18 |

Draw an ordered stem-and-leaf diagram to show this information.

(3 marks)

2 Edward asks 100 people how much they spent last year on newspapers. The results are given in the table below.

Amount £ (x)	Frequency
$0 \leqslant x < 10$	12
$10 \leqslant x < 20$	20
$20 \leqslant x < 30$	15
$30 \leqslant x < 40$	18
$40 \leqslant x < 50$	14
$50 \leqslant x < 60$	18
$60 \leqslant x < 70$	3

a) Calculate an estimate of the mean amount spent on newspapers.

(4 marks)

b) Explain briefly why this value of the mean is only an estimate.

(1 mark)

c) Calculate the class interval in which the median lies.

(2 marks)

d) Edward claims, 'The average amount of money spent on newspapers last year was between £10 and £20.' Explain whether you think that Edward's claim is correct.

(2 marks)

Score / 12

How well did you do?

| 0–7 Try again | 8–12 Getting there | 13–17 Good work | 18–23 Excellent! |

For more information on this topic, see pages 14–15 of your Success Revision Guide.

Probability 1

Multiple-choice questions

Choose just one answer, a, b, c or d. Circle your choice.

1) A bag of sweets contains five hard centres and three soft centres. What is the probability of choosing a hard centre if a sweet is picked out of the bag at random?

   a) $\frac{3}{5}$ b) $\frac{3}{8}$ c) $\frac{5}{8}$ d) $\frac{1}{2}$ (1 mark)

2) The probability that Highbury football club win a football match is $\frac{12}{17}$
   What is the probability that they do not win the football match?

   a) $\frac{5}{12}$ b) $\frac{17}{29}$ c) $\frac{12}{17}$ d) $\frac{5}{17}$ (1 mark)

3) A fair dice is thrown 600 times. On how many of these throws would you expect to get a 4?

   a) 40   b) 600   c) 100   d) 580   (1 mark)

4) A fair dice is thrown 500 times. If a 6 comes up 87 times, what is the relative frequency?

   a) $\frac{1}{6}$ b) $\frac{87}{500}$ c) $\frac{10}{600}$ d) $\frac{1}{587}$ (1 mark)

5) The probability that it will rain tomorrow is 0.35
   What is the probability that it will not rain tomorrow?

   a) 0.65   b) 0.35   c) 0.25   d) 1.35   (1 mark)

Score / 5

Short-answer questions

Answer all parts of each question.

1) The letters M A T H E M A T I C S are each placed on a separate piece of card and put into a bag. Stuart picks out a card at random. What is the probability he picks the following cards?

   a) The letter T _____   b) The letter M _____
   c) The letters A or C _____   d) The letter R _____   (4 marks)

2) The probability that George wins a tennis match is 0.6
   What is the probability that George does not win the tennis match? _____ (1 mark)

3) State whether each of these statements is **true** or **false**.

   a) The probability of getting a 6 when a fair dice is thrown is $\frac{1}{6}$ _____ (1 mark)

   b) The probability of passing a test in physics is 0.3
      If 100 students sit the test, the number expected to pass would be 3 _____ (1 mark)

   c) The probability that Conkers football team win a match is 0.8
      The probability that they will not win the game is 0.4 _____ (1 mark)

4) The probability of achieving a grade A in French is 0.2
   If 500 students sit the exam, how many students would you expect to achieve a grade A?
   _____ (2 marks)

Score /10

GCSE-style questions

Answer all parts of the questions. Show your workings (on a separate sheet of paper if necessary) and include the correct units in your answers.

1) A bag contains four blue, two green and six red counters. A counter is chosen at random from the bag.

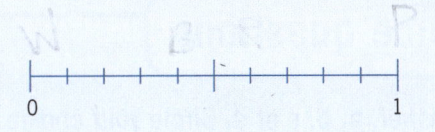

On the probability scale above…

a) label with the letter R the probability of choosing a red counter. **(1 mark)**

b) label with the letter B the probability of choosing a blue counter. **(1 mark)**

c) label with the letter W the probability of choosing a white counter. **(1 mark)**

d) label with the letter P the probability of choosing a blue, green or red counter. **(1 mark)**

2) There are 20 different-coloured sweets in a jar. The colour of each sweet can be red, green, yellow or blue. The table shows how many sweets of each colour are in the jar.

Colour	Red	Green	Yellow	Blue
Number	4	5	7	4

Reece picks one sweet at random from the jar.

a) Write down the probability that he will pick…

   i) a green sweet _____ ii) a yellow sweet. _____ **(2 marks)**

b) Write down the probability that he will not pick a blue sweet. _____ **(2 marks)**

3) A bag contains different beads of four different colours – red, white, blue and pink. The table shows the probability of taking a bead of a particular colour at random.

Colour	Red	White	Blue	Pink
Probability	0.25	0.1		0.3

Charlotte is going to take a bead at random and then put it back in the bag.

a) i) Work out the probability that Charlotte will take out a blue bead. _____ **(2 marks)**

   ii) Write down the probability that Charlotte will take out a black bead. _____ **(1 mark)**

b) Charlotte says there are exactly 12 counters in the bag. Charlotte is wrong. Explain why there cannot be exactly 12 counters in the bag.

_____ **(2 marks)**

c) Charlotte will take out a bead from the bag at random 200 times, replacing the bead each time. Work out an estimate for the number of times that Charlotte will take a red bead.

_____ **(2 marks)**

Score / 15

How well did you do?

0–6 Try again | 7–14 Getting there | 15–23 Good work | 24–30 Excellent!

For more information on this topic, see pages 16–17 of your Success Revision Guide.

Probability 2

Multiple-choice questions

Choose just one answer, a, b, c or d. Circle your choice.

1) Two dice are thrown and their scores are added. What is the probability of a score of 5?

   a) $\frac{1}{2}$ b) $\frac{2}{12}$ c) $\frac{4}{36}$ d) $\frac{5}{36}$ (1 mark)

2) Two dice are thrown and their scores are multiplied. What is the probability of a score of 1?

   a) $\frac{1}{36}$ b) $\frac{1}{12}$ c) $\frac{2}{12}$ d) $\frac{2}{36}$ (1 mark)

3) The probability that it snows on Christmas Day is 0.2
   What is the probability that it will not snow on Christmas Day?

   a) 0.8   b) 0.4   c) 0.16   d) 0.04   (1 mark)

4) The probability that Fiona is in the hockey team is 0.7
   What is the probability that Fiona is not in the hockey team?

   a) 1.7   b) 9.3   c) 0.7   d) 0.3   (1 mark)

Score   / 4

Short-answer questions

Answer all parts of each question.

Spinner 1: 3 3 / 2 1   Spinner 2: 6 2 / 3 1

1) Two spinners are spun at the same time and their scores are added.

   a) Complete the sample space diagram to show the possible outcomes.

   Spinner 1

	1	2	3	3
1	2			
2			5	
3		5		
6		8	9	

   Spinner 2

   (2 marks)

   b) Find the probability of…

   i) a score of 4 _____   ii) a score of 9 _____   iii) a score of 1 _____   (3 marks)

2) For lunch, Zi Ying has a sandwich and a drink. For her sandwich she can choose ham or cheese or beef. For her drink she can choose orange juice or tea. List all the possible lunches that Zi Ying can have.

   _____

   _____

   (2 marks)

Score   / 7

GCSE-style questions

Answer all parts of the questions. Show your workings (on a separate sheet of paper if necessary) and include the correct units in your answers.

1 Two fair dice are thrown together and their scores are added.

a) Work out the probability of a score of 7. _____ (2 marks)

b) Work out the probability of a score of 9. _____ (2 marks)

2 A youth club has 75 members. The table shows some information about the members.

	Under 13 years old	13 years and over	Total
Boys	15		42
Girls		21	
Total			75

a) Complete the table. (3 marks)

b) One of the club members is picked at random. Write down the probability that this member is under 13 years old.

_____ (1 mark)

3 a) Some students are given a choice of activities. In the morning they can do swimming (S), tennis (T) or art (A), and in the afternoon they have a choice of football (F) or swimming. Write down all the possible combinations that the students can choose if they do one activity in the morning and one activity in the afternoon.

_____
_____ (2 marks)

b) Assuming that all choices are equally likely, write down the probability that the students choose the same activity in the morning and afternoon.

_____ (1 mark)

Score / 11

How well did you do?

0–5 Try again | 6–11 Getting there | 12–18 Good work | 19–22 Excellent!

For more information on this topic, see pages 18–19 of your Success Revision Guide.

Number revision

Multiple-choice questions

Choose just one answer, a, b, c or d. Circle your choice.

1 Which of these is the largest number? 1469, 3271, 1059, 3276

   a) 1469   b) 3271   c) 1059   d) 3276

U2 (1 mark)

2 What does the digit 7 in the number 34 718 stand for?

   a) 7 units   b) 7 tens   c) 7 hundreds   d) 7 thousands

(1 mark)

3 Which number is fifty-two thousand, four hundred and six written in figures?

   a) 52 406   b) 54 206   c) 52 460   d) 5246

(1 mark)

4 What is the third multiple of 7?

   a) 7   b) 14   c) 21   d) 28

(1 mark)

5 Here are some cards. [3] [7] [6] [4]

   What is the **smallest** number you can make with these cards?

   a) 7643   b) 3764   c) 3674   d) 3467

(1 mark)

Score / 5

Short-answer questions

Answer all parts of each question.

1 What value does the digit 3 represent in each of these numbers?

   a) 739 _____

   b) 83 147 _____

   c) 346 295 _____

U2 (1 mark) (1 mark) (1 mark)

2 Write these numbers in words.

   a) 602 _____

   b) 5729 _____

(1 mark) (1 mark)

3 Write these numbers in figures.

   a) Four hundred and thirty-six _____

   b) Six million, four hundred and five _____

(1 mark) (1 mark)

4 Arrange these numbers in order of size, **smallest** first.

   a) 47, 6, 93, 827, 1436, 75, 102 _____

   b) 159, 3692, 4207, 4138, 729, 4879 _____

(2 marks) (2 marks)

Score / 11

GCSE-style questions

Answer all parts of the questions. Show your workings (on a separate sheet of paper if necessary) and include the correct units in your answers.

1 Here is a list of numbers.

17   170   1700   17 000   170 000   1 700 000

Write down the number from the list which is...

a) seventeen hundred .... (1 mark)

b) one hundred and seventy thousand .... (1 mark)

2 a) Write the number sixteen thousand, four hundred and thirty-one in figures.

.... (1 mark)

b) Write down the value of the 3 in the number 532 146.

.... (1 mark)

c) Write down the **smallest even number** that can be made from these cards.

3   5   2   8   .... (1 mark)

3 The table shows the amount of money raised from five charity events.

Charity event	Amount raised
Dance festival	£1061
Battle of the bands	£974
Sponsored run	£2712
Non-uniform day	£1361
Cake baking	£572

a) Write the amount of money raised at the dance festival in words.

.... (1 mark)

b) How much more did the sponsored run raise compared with the cake baking?

.... (2 marks)

4 a) Write these numbers in order of size, **smallest** first.

i) 61, 104, 18, 130, 72

.... (1 mark)

ii) 19, 62, 407, 397, 18

.... (1 mark)

b) How many numbers in the following list are multiples of 3?
5, 7, 8, 9, 11, 12, 13, 15, 16

.... (1 mark)

Score   / 11

How well did you do?

0–8 Try again   9–15 Getting there   16–22 Good work   23–27 Excellent!

For more information on this topic, see pages 22–23 of your Success Revision Guide.

Numbers

Multiple-choice questions

Choose just one answer, a, b, c or d. Circle your choice.

1) What is the positive square root of 81? **U2**
   a) 7   b) -9   c) -7   d) 9   (1 mark)

2) What is the value of 4^2?
   a) 12   b) 16   c) 4   d) 64   (1 mark)

3) Work out the value of $\sqrt[3]{27}$.
   a) 9   b) 6   c) 3   d) 81   (1 mark)

4) What is the highest common factor of 18 and 24?
   a) 6   b) 18   c) 12   d) 432   (1 mark)

5) What is the value of 4^3?
   a) 16   b) 64   c) 48   d) 2   (1 mark)

Score   / 5

Short-answer questions

Answer all parts of each question.

1) State whether each statement is **true** or **false**.   **U2**
   a) 2 is the only even prime number. _____ (1 mark)
   b) 12 is a factor of 6. _____ (1 mark)
   c) 9 is a factor of 3. _____ (1 mark)
   d) 1, 2, 4, 6, 12, 24 are the only factors of 24. _____ (1 mark)

2) Work out the answers to these questions.
   a) $\sqrt{4}$ = _____   b) $\sqrt{100}$ = _____   c) 4^3 = _____
   d) $\sqrt[3]{8}$ = _____   e) $\sqrt[3]{-125}$ = _____   f) 13^2 = _____   (6 marks)

3) Write 72 as a product of its prime factors. _____ (2 marks)

4) The number 180 is written as a product of its prime factors. What are the values of a and b?
   $180 = 2^a \times 3^b \times 5$ _____ (2 marks)

5) What is the least common multiple of 20 and 30? _____ (1 mark)

6) What is the highest common factor of 24 and 40? _____ (1 mark)

7) Decide whether this statement is **true** or **false**.
   75 written as a product of its prime factors is $3 \times 5 \times 5$ _____ (1 mark)

Score   / 17

GCSE-style questions

Answer all parts of the questions. Show your workings (on a separate sheet of paper if necessary) and include the correct units in your answers.

1 Some numbers are in the cloud below. Choose numbers from the cloud to answer the questions below.

9   6   16
1   12   17
11   25   24

a) Write down the square numbers. _____ (1 mark)

b) Write down the numbers that are factors of 24. _____ (2 marks)

c) Write down the prime numbers bigger than 7. _____ (1 mark)

2 a) Express the following numbers as products of their prime factors.

i) 56 _____ (2 marks)

ii) 60 _____ (2 marks)

b) Find the highest common factor of 56 and 60. _____ (2 marks)

c) Find the least common multiple of 56 and 60. _____ (2 marks)

3 The number 360 can be written as $2^a \times 3^b \times 5^c$

Calculate the values of a, b and c.

_____ (3 marks)

4 Susanne has a square patio of area $144m^2$. She uses $1m^2$ paving slabs. The paving slabs come in boxes of 20 and each box costs £30.

a) What is the length of Susanne's patio? _____ (2 marks)

b) How much will it cost Susanne to buy the paving slabs for her patio?

_____ (2 marks)

5 a is an even number, b is an odd number. Is ab an odd number, an even number or could it be either? Tick the correct box.

Odd number ☐   Even number ☐   Could be either ☐   (1 mark)

Score / 20

How well did you do?

0–11 Try again | 12–22 Getting there | 23–32 Good work | 33–42 Excellent!

For more information on this topic, see pages 22–23 of your Success Revision Guide.

Positive & negative numbers

Multiple-choice questions

Choose just one answer, a, b, c or d. Circle your choice.

1 If the numbers on the two cards are multiplied together, what is the answer?

-3   5

a) -15   b) 2   c) 15   d) 8   (1 mark)

2 What is the value of -12 + (-6)?

a) -6   b) -20   c) 6   d) -18   (1 mark)

3 Here are some number cards. Which two number cards add up to give 1?

-7   4   9   -3

a) -7 and 4   b) 4 and -3   c) 9 and 4   d) -7 and -3   (1 mark)

4 Which number in this list is the **largest**? 7, 11, -20, -41

a) 7   b) 11   c) -20   d) -41   (1 mark)

5 The temperature outside is -5°C. Inside it is 28 degrees warmer. What is the temperature inside?

a) 17°C   b) 21°C   c) 23°C   d) 25°C   (1 mark)

Score / 5

Short-answer questions

Answer all parts of each question.

1 Here are some number cards: -7   0   5   -3

a) Choose two of the number cards that add up to give -2. _____ (1 mark)

b) Choose two of the number cards that subtract to give -4. _____ (1 mark)

c) Choose two of the number cards that multiply to give -15. _____ (1 mark)

2 Draw a line to join each calculation to the correct answer.

-3 × 4   10
12 ÷ (-2)   -1
-4 – (-3)   -12
-5 × (-2)   4
-20 ÷ (-5)   -6

(5 marks)

3 Work out the answers to the following questions.

a) (-40) ÷ (-4) = _____   b) -7 + (-3) = _____   c) 8 – (-6) = _____

(3 marks)

Score / 11

GCSE-style questions

Answer all parts of the questions. Show your workings (on a separate sheet of paper if necessary) and include the correct units in your answers.

1 The temperatures at midnight in various cities on one night in December are shown in the table opposite.

City	Temperature (°C)
Cairo	4
London	-2
New York	-7
Oslo	-14

a) How many degrees warmer is Cairo than Oslo? _____ ° (1 mark)

b) i) On the same night, the temperature in Sydney is 24 degrees warmer than in New York. What is the temperature in Sydney?

_____ °C (2 marks)

ii) How many degrees colder is it in London than in Sydney?

_____ ° (2 marks)

2 One evening last winter, the temperature in Swansea was 4°C, in Manchester it was -2°C and in Glasgow it was -8°C.

a) Work out the difference in temperature between Swansea and Glasgow.

_____ ° (1 mark)

b) The temperature in Manchester increased by 6 degrees. Work out the new temperature in Manchester.

_____ °C (1 mark)

c) The temperature in Glasgow fell by 3 degrees. Work out the new temperature in Glasgow.

_____ °C (1 mark)

3 Place these numbers in order of size, smallest first.

-4   9   -2   1   0   8   -13   -5

_____ _____ _____ _____ _____ _____ _____ _____ (2 marks)

4 Here are some numbers in a number pyramid. The number in each rectangle is found by adding the two numbers below. What are the values of w, x and y?

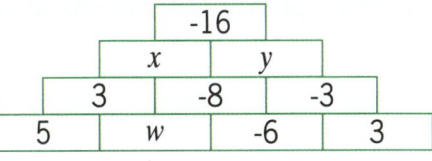

```
            -16
         x      y
      3    -8    -3
    5    w    -6    3
```

(3 marks)

Score ___ / 13

How well did you do?

| 0–6 | Try again | 7–14 | Getting there | 15–23 | Good work | 24–29 | Excellent! |

For more information on this topic, see pages 24–25 of your Success Revision Guide.

Working with numbers

Multiple-choice questions

Choose just one answer, a, b, c or d. Circle your choice.

1 Work out the answer to 27 × 100

a) 27   b) 2700   c) 270   d) 27 000

U2 (1 mark)

2 Work out the answer to 81 ÷ 1000

a) 81   b) 0.81   c) 0.081   d) 8.1

(1 mark)

3 Work out the answer to 274 + 639

a) 913   b) 931   c) 879   d) 874

(1 mark)

4 Work out the answer to 1479 – 387

a) 1192   b) 1092   c) 1112   d) 1012

(1 mark)

5 Work out the answer to 379 × 6

a) 2072   b) 2174   c) 3274   d) 2274

(1 mark)

Score / 5

Short-answer questions

Answer all parts of each question.

1 Draw a line from each calculation to the correct answer.

6 × 10	2400
70 × 1000	70 000
240 ÷ 100	60
600 ÷ 1000	2.4
80 × 30	0.6

U2

(5 marks)

2 Work out the following calculations, showing all your working.

a) 379 + 42 = ...   b) 639 – 274 = ...

c) 5296 × 3 = ...   d) 2496 ÷ 3 = ...

(4 marks)

3 Work out the following calculations, showing all your working.

a) 279 × 26 = ...   b) 159 × 48 = ...

c) 323 ÷ 19 = ...   d) 1296 ÷ 27 = ...

(4 marks)

4 A shop buys 142 sweaters. If each sweater is sold for £62, how much money does the shop take in total?

....

£ ....

(2 marks)

Score / 15

GCSE-style questions

Answer all parts of the questions. Show your workings (on a separate sheet of paper if necessary) and include the correct units in your answers.

1 a) Here is Gill's shopping bill. Complete the totals.

Item	Cost	Number bought	Total cost
Bread	79p	4	
Milk	72p	2	
Cleaning fluid	£2.76	2	

(3 marks)

b) Gill pays using a £5 voucher and the remainder in cash. How much cash does she pay?

(1 mark)

2 Mrs Sharpe is printing a test for all year 10 students. Each test uses 16 sheets of paper.

a) There are 186 students in year 10. How many sheets of paper does she need?

(3 marks)

b) A ream contains 500 sheets of paper. How many reams of paper does she need to print all the tests?

(2 marks)

3 The table shows the cost of three types of pen. Simon buys one gel pen and one roller-ball pen. He pays with a £10 note.

Gel pen	£2.15
Fibre-tip pen	£2.00
Roller-ball pen	£2.70

a) How much change should he get?

(4 marks)

b) Shezad wants to buy some fibre-tip pens. He has £25 to spend. What is the greatest number of fibre-tip pens he can buy?

(2 marks)

4 Three teachers are planning to take some students to the zoo. Adult tickets cost £20 and student tickets cost £15. There is a budget of £560 for the tickets. Work out the greatest number of students that can go to the zoo.

(3 marks)

Score / 18

How well did you do?

0–13 Try again | 14–22 Getting there | 23–32 Good work | 33–38 Excellent!

For more information on this topic, see pages 26–27 of your Success Revision Guide.

Fractions

Multiple-choice questions

Choose just one answer, a, b, c or d. Circle your choice.

1 In a class of 24 students, $\frac{3}{8}$ wear glasses. How many students wear glasses?   [U1 | U2 | U3]

a) 9   b) 6   c) 3   d) 12   (1 mark)

2 Work out the answer to $\frac{5}{9} - \frac{1}{3}$.   [U2]

a) $\frac{1}{3}$ b) $\frac{2}{9}$ c) $\frac{4}{6}$ d) $\frac{4}{12}$ (1 mark)

3 Work out the answer to $\frac{2}{11} \times \frac{7}{9}$

a) $\frac{14}{11}$ b) $\frac{14}{9}$ c) $\frac{14}{99}$ d) $\frac{2}{99}$ (1 mark)

4 Work out the answer to $\frac{3}{10} \div \frac{2}{5}$

a) $\frac{3}{4}$ b) $\frac{6}{50}$ c) $\frac{6}{15}$ d) $\frac{4}{3}$ (1 mark)

5 Which one of these fractions is equivalent to $\frac{5}{9}$?   [U2 | U3]

a) $\frac{16}{27}$ b) $\frac{9}{18}$ c) $\frac{25}{45}$ d) $\frac{21}{36}$ (1 mark)

Score / 5

Short-answer questions

Answer all parts of each question.

1 Arrange these fractions in order of size, **smallest** first. (Hint: change the fractions so that the denominators are the same where appropriate.)   [U1 | U2]

a) $\frac{2}{3}$ $\frac{4}{5}$ $\frac{3}{4}$ $\frac{1}{2}$ $\frac{3}{10}$

(2 marks)

b) $\frac{5}{8}$ $\frac{1}{3}$ $\frac{1}{9}$ $\frac{3}{4}$ $\frac{2}{5}$

(2 marks)

2 State whether these statements are **true** or **false**.

a) $\frac{4}{5}$ of 20 is bigger than $\frac{6}{7}$ of 14. ....   (1 mark)

b) $\frac{2}{9}$ of 27 is smaller than $\frac{1}{3}$ of 15. ....   (1 mark)

3 Work out the answers to the following. Give your answer in the simplest form.   [U2]

a) $\frac{2}{9} + \frac{1}{3}$ ....   b) $\frac{7}{11} - \frac{1}{4}$ ....   c) $\frac{4}{7} \times \frac{3}{8}$ ....   d) $\frac{9}{12} \div \frac{1}{4}$ ....

e) $\frac{5}{7} - \frac{1}{21}$ ....   f) $\frac{4}{9} + \frac{3}{27}$ ....   g) $\frac{7}{12} \times \frac{3}{2}$ ....   h) $\frac{11}{7} \div \frac{12}{7}$ ....   (8 marks)

4 Change these improper fractions to mixed numbers.

a) $\frac{5}{2} =$ ....   b) $\frac{5}{3} =$ ....

c) $\frac{9}{2} =$ ....   d) $\frac{12}{11} =$ ....   (4 marks)

Short-answer questions (cont.)

5 Fill in the blanks in these equivalent fractions.

a) $\frac{2}{11} = \frac{4}{\_\_}$ b) $\frac{4}{7} = \frac{\_\_}{49}$ c) $\frac{25}{100} = \frac{1}{\_\_}$ d) $\frac{12}{17} = \frac{36}{\_\_}$

U2 U3
(4 marks)

Score / 22

GCSE-style questions

Answer all parts of the questions. Show your workings (on a separate sheet of paper if necessary) and include the correct units in your answers.

1 In a class of 32 pupils, $\frac{1}{8}$ are left-handed. How many students are not left-handed?

U1 U2
(1 mark)

2 Reece works 15 hours per week. He earns £6 per hour. Reece saves $\frac{1}{5}$ of his earnings each week. He needs to save £120 for a holiday. How many weeks does it take Reece to save £120?

(4 marks)

3 Gill is 56. Her son Steve is $\frac{5}{8}$ of her age. Her grand-daughter Jessica is $\frac{1}{7}$ of her age. How many years older than Jessica is Steve?

(4 marks)

4 Work out these.

a) $\frac{2}{3} + \frac{4}{5}$ _____ (1 mark)

b) $\frac{9}{11} - \frac{1}{3}$ _____ (1 mark)

c) $\frac{2}{7} \times \frac{4}{9}$ _____ (1 mark)

d) $\frac{3}{10} \div \frac{2}{5}$ _____ (1 mark)

U2

5 Charlotte's take-home pay is £930. She gives her mother $\frac{1}{3}$ of this and spends $\frac{1}{5}$ of the £930 on going out. What fraction of the £930 is left? Give your answer as a fraction in its simplest form.

(3 marks)

6 Phoebe says, 'Since 5 is halfway between 4 and 6 then $\frac{1}{5}$ will be halfway between $\frac{1}{4}$ and $\frac{1}{6}$.' Phoebe is wrong. Show that $\frac{1}{5}$ is not halfway between $\frac{1}{4}$ and $\frac{1}{6}$.

(3 marks)

7 A metal rod weighs $3\frac{1}{2}$kg. A packing crate weighs $10\frac{1}{2}$kg. 30 rods are packed into the crate. What is the total weight of the rods and the crate?

(3 marks)

Score / 22

How well did you do?

| 0–14 Try again | 15–27 Getting there | 28–39 Good work | 40–49 Excellent! |

For more information on this topic, see pages 28–29 of your Success Revision Guide.

Decimals

Multiple-choice questions

Choose just one answer, a, b, c or d. Circle your choice.

1 Here are some discs. ⟨5.8⟩ ⟨5.79⟩ ⟨5.81⟩ ⟨5.805⟩

Which of these discs has the **largest** number?

a) 5.8   b) 5.79   c) 5.81   d) 5.805   (1 mark)

2 Round 18.629 to 2 decimal places.

a) 18.69   b) 18.63   c) 18.7   d) 18.62   (1 mark)

3 Work out the answer to 9.45 × 5

a) 47.52   b) 56.7   c) 47.25   d) 46.75   (1 mark)

4 If a piece of cheese weighs 0.3kg, how much would 70 identical pieces of cheese weigh?

a) 2.1kg   b) 21kg   c) 0.21kg   d) 210kg   (1 mark)

5 Work out the answer to 520 ÷ 0.02

a) 2600   b) 260   c) 260 000   d) 26 000   (1 mark)

Score / 5

Short-answer questions

Answer all parts of each question.

1 Four friends run a race. Their times in seconds are shown in the table below.

Thomas	Hussain	Molly	Joshua
14.072	15.12	14.07	16.321

a) Who won the race? _____ (1 mark)

b) What is the difference between Hussain and Joshua's times? _____ (1 mark)

c) How much faster was Molly than Thomas? _____ (1 mark)

2 Look at these statements and decide whether they are **true** or **false**.

a) 0.72 is greater than 0.724 _____ (1 mark)

b) 6.427 rounded to 2 decimal places is 6.43 _____ (1 mark)

c) 27.406 rounded to 2 decimal places is 27.41 _____ (1 mark)

3 Here are some calculations. Fill in the gaps to make the calculations correct.

a) 640 ÷ 40 = _____   b) 500 × 0.2 = _____   c) 600 ÷ 0.3 = _____

d) 40 ÷ _____ = 400   e) _____ × 0.02 = 0.48   f) 420 ÷ _____ = 42 000

(6 marks)

Score / 12

GCSE-style questions

Answer all parts of the questions. Show your workings (on a separate sheet of paper if necessary) and include the correct units in your answers.

1 a) Ryan has three pounds and forty pence. His friend, Dom, has two pounds and three pence. Write down in figures how much money Ryan and Dom each have.

Ryan: £ _____   Dom: £ _____

(U1)

(2 marks)

b) Ryan writes down the total amount of money that he and Dom have as £5.7, but he is wrong. Explain why Ryan is wrong.

_____

(2 marks)

2 Here are some number cards. (6.14) (7.29) (7.42) (7.208) (6.141)

a) Arrange the cards in order of size, **smallest** first.

( ) ( ) ( ) ( ) ( )

(U1 | U2)

(2 marks)

b) Work out the difference between the largest and the smallest number.

_____

(1 mark)

c) What is the total of all these cards? _____

(1 mark)

d) Round these cards to 2 decimal places.

(7.208) (6.141)

i) 7.208 becomes _____   ii) 6.141 becomes _____

(2 marks)

3 a) Write the number 0.313 as a fraction.

_____

(1 mark)

b) Write $\frac{11}{20}$ as a decimal. _____

(1 mark)

4 Here are some number cards.

(0.1) (0.01) (0.001) (100) (10)

Use one of the number cards to fill each gap to make the calculations correct.

a) 60 ÷ _____ = 6000

(1 mark)

b) 25 × _____ = 2.5

(1 mark)

c) 720 ÷ _____ = 720 000

(1 mark)

(U2)

5 Matthew is putting a new fence down the side of his garden. The fence panels are 0.9 metres long. The total length of the fence needs to be 5.4 metres. Each fence panel costs £17.48. Work out how much it costs Matthew to put the fence down the side of his garden.

£ _____

(4 marks)

Score ___ / 19

How well did you do?

0–9 Try again | 10–18 Getting there | 19–28 Good work | 29–36 Excellent!

For more information on this topic, see pages 30–31 of your Success Revision Guide.

Percentages 1

Multiple-choice questions

Choose just one answer, a, b, c or d. Circle your choice.

1 Work out 10% of £850.

a) £8.50   b) £0.85   c) £85   d) £42.50   (1 mark)

2 Work out 17.5% of £60.

a) £9   b) £15   c) £10.50   d) £12.50   (1 mark)

3 A CD player costs £45. In a sale, the price is reduced by 20%. What is the sale price of the CD player?

a) £38   b) £40.50   c) £9   d) £36   (1 mark)

4 A television costs £1200. In a sale, it is reduced by 15%. What is the sale price of the television?

a) £960   b) £180   c) £240   d) £1020   (1 mark)

5 In a survey, 17 people out of 25 said they preferred type A cola. What percentage of people preferred type A cola?

a) 68%   b) 60%   c) 72%   d) 75%   (1 mark)

Score / 5

Short-answer questions

Answer all parts of each question.

1 Last year, Colin earned £25 500. This year he has a 3% pay rise. How much does Colin now earn?

£ ....   (2 marks)

2 A coat costs £120. In a sale, it is reduced by 15%. Work out the sale price of the coat.

£ ....   (2 marks)

3 Lucinda scored 58 out of 75 in a test. What percentage did she get? Give your answer to the nearest whole number.

.... %   (2 marks)

4 The cost of a train ticket was £11.20. The price of the ticket rose by 7%. What is the cost of the train ticket after the price increase?

£ ....   (2 marks)

5 12 out of 30 people wear glasses. What percentage wear glasses?

.... %   (2 marks)

Short-answer questions (cont.)

6 Draw a line from each calculation to the correct answer.

10% of 30   16

40% of 40   5

5% of 15   3

25% of 20   0.75

(4 marks)

Score   / 14

GCSE-style questions

Answer all parts of the questions. Show your workings (on a separate sheet of paper if necessary) and include the correct units in your answers.

1 The table shows Bibi's results in two maths tests.

In which test did Bibi do better? Show your working.

Test	Mark
1	70 out of 90
2	36 out of 48

U1

_____

(3 marks)

2 Ruby sells some books. She sells each book for £7.80 plus VAT at 17.5%. She sells 470 books. Work out how much money Ruby receives.

£ _____

(4 marks)

3 Rosie sees an advert for a summer holiday.

Prices are per person.

Arabian Specials

Dates	7 Nights	10 Nights	Child Price
1–10 May	£861	£984	£399
11–22 May	£831	£940	£399
23–28 May	£946	£1162	£399

Rosie books a holiday online for two adults and three children. They travel on May 24th and stay for 7 nights. When booking online, you receive a percentage reduction. Rosie's final bill is £2718.32. What was the percentage reduction for booking online?

_____ %

(5 marks)

4 The price of a television set is £175 plus VAT at 17.5%. Work out the amount of VAT charged.

£ _____

U2

(2 marks)

5 In a sale, normal prices are reduced by 15%. The normal price of a washing machine is £400. Work out the sale price of the washing machine.

£ _____

(3 marks)

Score   / 17

How well did you do?

| 0–9 | Try again | 10–17 | Getting there | 18–27 | Good work | 28–36 | Excellent! |

For more information on this topic, see pages 32–33 of your Success Revision Guide.

Percentages 2

Multiple-choice questions

Choose just one answer, a, b, c or d. Circle your choice.

1) £2000 is invested in a savings account. Simple interest is paid at 2.1%. How much interest is paid after one year?

   a) £4   b) £5.20   c) £42   d) £84.88   (1 mark)

2) Lucy earns £23 500. National Insurance (NI) is deducted at 11%. How much NI must she pay?

   a) £2250   b) £2585   c) £2605   d) £21 385   (1 mark)

3) A bike was bought for £120. Each year its value depreciated by 10%. What was the bike worth one year later?

   a) £108   b) £106   c) £132   d) £110   (1 mark)

Score / 3

Short-answer questions

Answer all parts of each question.

1) A meal costs £143. VAT at 17.5% is added to the price of the meal. What is the final price of the meal?

   £ _____ (2 marks)

2) VAT of 5% is added to a gas bill of £72. Find the total amount to be paid.

   £ _____ (2 marks)

3) A motorbike is bought for £9000. Each year it depreciates in value by 12%. Work out the value of the motorbike after one year.

   £ _____ (2 marks)

4) A computer is bought for £800. Each year it depreciates in value by 30%. Work out the value of the computer after one year.

   £ _____ (2 marks)

5) A house was bought for £200 000. Five years later it was sold for £250 000. What is the percentage profit?

   _____ % (2 marks)

6) Jack bought a motorbike for £15 000. He later sold it for £12 000. What is the percentage loss?

   _____ % (2 marks)

Score / 12

GCSE-style questions

Answer all parts of the questions. Show your workings (on a separate sheet of paper if necessary) and include the correct units in your answers.

1 A year ago Matthew's height was 1.43 metres. His height has now increased by 12.3%. Work out Matthew's height now. Give your answer to an appropriate degree of accuracy.

U1

(3 marks)

2 Here is part of Melissa's gas bill.

> **Gas Bill**
> New Reading: 5838
> Old Reading: 2715
> Cost per unit: 3.64p
> VAT at 5%

Work out the total cost of the gas, including VAT at 5%.

£..................

(5 marks)

3 Work out 40% of £2500.

£..................

U2

(2 marks)

4 Find the simple interest on £2000 invested for two years at 4% per year.

£..................

(3 marks)

5 Last year, Rupinder earned £26 500. She does not have to pay income tax on £9500 of these earnings of £26 500. She has to pay income tax at 20% on all her earnings above £9500. Work out how much income tax Rupinder has to pay.

£..................

(3 marks)

6 Richard is buying a car for £8000. He pays a 20% deposit and then takes out a loan for the rest of the payment. The loan is charged at an interest rate of 7.5% per year. Richard intends to pay back the loan in one year. How much does Richard pay for the car?

£..................

(3 marks)

7 A shop is selling a racing bike for the cash price of £1350. You can also buy it on credit for a 30% deposit plus 24 monthly payments of £50. How much more does it cost to buy the bike on credit rather than paying cash?

£..................

(4 marks)

Score / 23

How well did you do?

| 0–9 Try again | 10–16 Getting there | 17–28 Good work | 29–38 Excellent! |

For more information on this topic, see pages 34–35 of your Success Revision Guide.

Fractions, decimals & percentages

Multiple-choice questions

Choose just one answer, a, b, c or d. Circle your choice.

1 What is $\frac{3}{5}$ as a percentage?

  a) 30%   b) 25%   c) 60%   d) 75%

U1 U2 U3 (1 mark)

2 What is $\frac{2}{3}$ written as a decimal?

  a) 0.77   b) $0.\dot{6}$ c) 0.665   d) 0.6

(1 mark)

3 What is the **smallest** value in this list of numbers? 29%, 0.4, $\frac{3}{4}$, $\frac{1}{8}$

  a) 29%   b) 0.4   c) $\frac{3}{4}$ d) $\frac{1}{8}$

(1 mark)

4 What is the **largest** value in this list of numbers? $\frac{4}{5}$, 80%, $\frac{2}{3}$, 0.9

  a) $\frac{4}{5}$ b) 80%   c) $\frac{2}{3}$ d) 0.9

(1 mark)

5 Change $\frac{5}{8}$ into a decimal.

  a) 0.625   b) 0.425   c) 0.125   d) 0.725

U1 U3 (1 mark)

Score / 5

Short-answer questions

Answer all parts of each question.

1 The table shows equivalent fractions, decimals and percentages. Fill in the gaps.

U1 U2 U3

Fraction	Decimal	Percentage
$\frac{2}{5}$		
		5%
	$0.\dot{3}$	
	0.04	
		25%
$\frac{1}{8}$		

(6 marks)

2 Put these cards in order of size, **smallest** first.

0.37   30% $\frac{3}{8}$ $\frac{1}{3}$ 92% $\frac{1}{2}$ 0.62

◯ ◯ ◯ ◯ ◯ ◯ ◯

(2 marks)

Short-answer questions (cont.)

3 A sundial is being sold in two different garden centres. The cost of the sundial is £89.99 in both garden centres. Both garden centres have a promotion.

Gardens Are Us — Sundial 22% off

Rosebushes — Sundial $\frac{1}{4}$ off

In which garden centre is the sundial **cheaper**? Explain your answer.

(2 marks)

Score / 10

GCSE-style questions

Answer all parts of the questions. Show your workings (on a separate sheet of paper if necessary) and include the correct units in your answers.

1 Philippa is buying a new television. She sees three different advertisements for the same television set.

Ed's Electricals
TV normal price
£250
Sale 10% off

Sheila's Bargains
TV £185 plus VAT at $17\frac{1}{2}$%

GITA's TV SHOP
Normal price
£290
Sale: $\frac{1}{5}$ off normal price

Philippa wants to buy her television from one of these shops, as cheaply as possible. Which shop should she choose and how much cheaper is it than the most expensive shop?

(5 marks)

2 Place these seven numbers in order of size, **smallest** first.

25%, $\frac{1}{3}$, 0.27, $\frac{2}{5}$, 0.571, 72%, $\frac{1}{8}$

(3 marks)

3 Decide whether these calculations give the same answer for this instruction: increase £40 by 20%.

Jack says: Multiply 40 by 1.2

Hannah says: Work out 10%, double it and then add 40

Explain your reasoning.

(2 marks)

Score / 10

How well did you do?

0–7 Try again | 8–13 Getting there | 14–20 Good work | 21–25 Excellent!

For more information on this topic, see page 36 of your Success Revision Guide.

Approximating & using a calculator

Multiple-choice questions

Choose just one answer, a, b, c or d. Circle your choice.

1 Round 5379 to 1 significant figure.
 a) 500   b) 50   c) 5   d) 5000   (1 mark)

2 Estimate the answer to the calculation 27 × 41
 a) 1107   b) 1200   c) 820   d) 1300   (1 mark)

3 A carton of orange juice costs 79p. Estimate the cost of 402 cartons of orange juice.
 a) £350   b) £250   c) £400   d) £320   (1 mark)

4 A school trip is organised. 407 pupils are going on the trip. Each coach seats 50 pupils. Approximately how many coaches are needed?
 a) 12   b) 5   c) 8   d) 10   (1 mark)

5 Estimate the answer to the calculation $\frac{(4.2)^2}{107}$
 a) 16   b) 1.6   c) 0.16   d) 160   (1 mark)

Score / 5

Short-answer questions

Answer all parts of each question.

1 State whether each statement is **true** or **false**.
 a) 2.742 rounded to 1 significant figure is 3   (1 mark)
 b) 2793 rounded to 1 significant figure is 2800   (1 mark)
 c) 32 046 rounded to 1 significant figure is 40 000   (1 mark)
 d) 14.637 rounded to 1 significant figure is 10   (1 mark)

2 Work out the following on your calculator. Write down all the figures on your calculator display.
 a) $\frac{4.2 \times (3.6 + 5.1)}{2 - 1.9}$ b) $6 \times \sqrt{\frac{12.1}{4.2}}$
 c) $\frac{12^5}{4.3 \times 9.15}$ (3 marks)

3 Round each of the numbers in the following calculations to 1 significant figure, then work out an approximate answer.
 a) $\frac{(32.9)^2}{9.1}$ (1 mark)
 b) $\frac{(906 \div 31.4)^2}{7.1 + 2.9}$ (1 mark)

Short-answer questions (cont.)

4 Tim works in a bookshop. He earns £5.95 per hour. One week, Tim works 21 hours. Approximately how much does Tim earn in that week?

U2

(2 marks)

Score / 11

GCSE-style questions

Answer all parts of the questions. Show your workings (on a separate sheet of paper if necessary) and include the correct units in your answers.

1 Use your calculator to work out the value of the following. Write down all the figures on your calculator display.

$$\frac{\sqrt{4.9^2 + 6.3}}{2.1 \times 0.37}$$

U1 U3

(3 marks)

2 a) Use your calculator to work out the value of the following. Write down all the figures on your calculator display.

$$\frac{27.1 \times 6.2}{38.2 - 9.9}$$

(2 marks)

b) Round each of the numbers in the above calculation to 1 significant figure and obtain an approximate answer.

(3 marks)

3 a) Use your calculator to work out the value of the following. Write down all the figures on your calculator display.

$$\frac{(15.2 + 6.9)^2}{3.63 - 4.2}$$

(2 marks)

b) Round your answer to 1 significant figure. (1 mark)

4 a) Write down two numbers you could use to get an approximate answer to 31×79.

U2

_____ and _____ (1 mark)

b) Work out your approximate answer. _____ (1 mark)

c) Work out the difference between your approximate answer and the exact answer.

(2 marks)

5 Estimate the answer to the following. Leave your answer as an improper fraction in its simplest form.

$$\frac{21.2^2 - 10.3^2}{3.6 \times 29}$$

(3 marks)

Score / 18

How well did you do?

| 0–10 Try again | 11–16 Getting there | 17–23 Good work | 24–34 Excellent! |

For more information on this topic, see pages 37–41 of your Success Revision Guide.

Ratio

Multiple-choice questions

Choose just one answer, a, b, c or d. Circle your choice.

1) What is the ratio 6 : 18 written in its simplest form?
   a) 3 : 1   b) 3 : 9   c) 1 : 3   d) 9 : 3   (1 mark)   U1

2) Write the ratio 200 : 500 in its simplest form.
   a) 20 : 50   b) 1 : 5   c) 1 : 25   d) 2 : 5   (1 mark)

3) A recipe for 4 people needs 800g of flour. How much flour is needed for 6 people?
   a) 12g   b) 120g   c) 12kg   d) 1200g   (1 mark)   U1 U2

4) If 9 oranges cost £1.08, how much would 14 similar oranges cost?
   a) £1.50   b) £1.68   c) £1.20   d) £1.84   (1 mark)

5) If £140 is divided in the ratio 3 : 4, what is the size of the larger share?
   a) £45   b) £60   c) £80   d) £90   (1 mark)   U2

Score / 5

Short-answer questions

Answer all parts of each question.

1) Write down each of the following ratios in the form $1 : n$ U1
   a) 10 : 30 _____   b) 6 : 24 _____   c) 9 : 27 _____   (3 marks)

2) 7 bottles of lemonade have a total capacity of 1680ml. Work out the total capacity of 5 similar bottles.
   _____ ml   (1 mark)

3) It takes 6 people 3 days to dig and lay a cable. How long would it take 4 people? (All people work at the same rate.)   U1 U2
   _____ days   (2 marks)

4) If £1 = 1.09 euros (€), change €726 into pounds. Give your answer to the nearest penny.   U1 U3
   £ _____   (2 marks)

5) a) Increase £4.10 in the ratio 2 : 5   U2
      £ _____   (1 mark)
   b) Decrease 120g in the ratio 5 : 2 _____ g   (1 mark)

6) Mrs London inherited £88 000. She divided the money between her children in the ratio 3 : 3 : 5. How much did the child with the largest share receive?
   £ _____   (2 marks)

Score / 12

GCSE-style questions

Answer all parts of the questions. Show your workings (on a separate sheet of paper if necessary) and include the correct units in your answers.

1 James uses these ingredients to make 12 buns:

> 50g butter, 40g sugar, 2 eggs, 45g flour, 15ml milk

James wants to make 30 similar buns. Write down how much of each ingredient he needs for 30 buns.

Butter _____ g

Sugar _____ g

Eggs _____

Flour _____ g

Milk _____ ml

(U1 U2)

(3 marks)

2 It takes 3 builders 16 days to build a wall. All the builders work at the same rate. How long would it take 8 builders to build a wall of the same size?

_____ days

(3 marks)

3 7 metres of rope costs £5.46. Work out the cost of 13 metres of the same rope.

£ _____

(U1 U3)

(2 marks)

4 Vicky and Tracy share £14 400 in the ratio 4 : 5. How much does each of them receive?

Vicky: £ _____   Tracy: £ _____

(U2)

(3 marks)

5 Sahil invests some money in a savings account (SA) and in a cash ISA (I). The ratio of the amounts of money invested is SA : I = 5 : 7. He invests £2800 in the cash ISA. How much money does he invest altogether?

£ _____

(2 marks)

6 Mineral water is sold in two sizes.

Which size bottle gives the better value for money? You must show all of your working. 🖩

Water 1 litre — £1.52

Water 25cl — 61p

(U3)

(2 marks)

Score ___ / 15

How well did you do?

| 0–6 Try again | 7–14 Getting there | 15–23 Good work | 24–32 Excellent! |

For more information on this topic, see pages 42–43 of your Success Revision Guide.

Indices

Multiple-choice questions

Choose just one answer, a, b, c or d. Circle your choice.

1 In index form, what is the value of $8^3 \times 8^{11}$?

   a) 8^{14} b) 8^{33} c) 64^{14} d) 64^{33} (1 mark)

2 In index form, what is the value of $4^2 \times 4^3$?

   a) 12^2 b) 4^5 c) 4^6 d) 16^6 (1 mark)

3 What is the value of 5^0?

   a) 5   b) 0   c) 25   d) 1   (1 mark)

4 What is the value of $2^3 \times 3^2$?

   a) 36   b) 54   c) 48   d) 72   (1 mark)

5 What is the value of $7^{12} \div 7^2$ written in index form?

   a) 7^{10} b) 7^6 c) 7^{14} d) 7^{24} (1 mark)

Score / 5

Short-answer questions

Answer all parts of each question.

1 Work out the exact value of these.

   a) 4^3 b) 2^5 c) 3^4 (3 marks)

2 Decide whether each of these expressions is **true** or **false**.

   a) $a^4 \times a^5 = a^{20}$ b) $2a^4 \times 3a^2 = 5a^8$

   c) $10a^6 \div 2a^4 = 5a^2$ d) $20a^4b^2 \div 10a^5b = \dfrac{2b}{a}$

   e) $7^3 \times 7^4 = 7^{12}$ f) $2a^9 \times 3a = 6a^{10}$ (6 marks)

3 Simplify the following expressions.

   a) $3a \times 2a =$ b) $12m^3 \div 4m =$

   c) $10a^2b^4 \times 2ab =$ d) $n^7 \times n^9 =$

   e) $a^{12} \div a =$ f) $32a^{14} \div 16a^7 =$

   g) $4a^5 \times 3a^6 =$ h) $12b^3 \div 4b =$ (8 marks)

4 Find the value of n in each of the following equations.

   a) $8^{10} \times 8^n = 8^{16}$ b) $10^n \div 10^2 = 10^{12}$

   c) $5^n = 5$ d) $a^n \div a^4 = a^{12}$ (4 marks)

Score / 21

GCSE-style questions

Answer all parts of the questions. Show your workings (on a separate sheet of paper if necessary) and include the correct units in your answers.

1 Michelle says that $m^3 \times m^2 = m^6$. Michelle is wrong. Explain why Michelle is wrong. (U2)
(2 marks)

2 a) Work out the value of the following:

i) 4^2 ii) 3^3 (2 marks)

b) Write the following as a power of 9: $9 \times 9 \times 9 \times 9 \times 9$ (1 mark)

3 Simplify the following:

a) $p^3 \times p^4$ (1 mark)

b) $\dfrac{n^{10}}{n^7}$ (1 mark)

c) $\dfrac{a^3 \times a^4}{a}$ (1 mark)

d) $\dfrac{12a^2b}{3a}$ (1 mark)

e) $5n^6 \times 2n^5$ (1 mark)

4 Work out the value of the following:

a) 3^1 **b)** 5^2 (2 marks)

c) $3^4 \times 2^3$ (1 mark)

5 a) Evaluate the following:

i) 8^1 ii) 6^2 (2 marks)

iii) $2^3 \times 2^2$ (1 mark)

b) Write this expression as a single power of 5:

$\dfrac{5^7 \times 5^3}{5^6}$ (2 marks)

6 Simplify the following:

a) $2a^3 \times 3a^2$ **b)** $\dfrac{12a^2b}{4ab}$ (2 marks)

c) $\dfrac{b^6 \times 3b^2}{12b^{10}}$ **d)** $2x^3 \times 4x^3$ (2 marks)

7 Evaluate the following:

a) i) 7^2 ii) $3^2 \times 3^3$ iii) $4^7 \div 4^5$ (3 marks)

b) Write $\dfrac{3^4 \times 3^6}{3^2}$ as a single power of 3. (2 marks)

Score / 27

How well did you do?

0–13 Try again 14–26 Getting there 27–41 Good work 42–53 Excellent!

For more information on this topic, see pages 44–45 of your Success Revision Guide.

43

Algebra

Multiple-choice questions

Choose just one answer, a, b, c or d. Circle your choice.

1) What is the expression $4a + 3b - a + 6b$ when it is fully simplified? [U2|U3]
  a) $9b - 3a$ b) $3a9b$ c) $3a + 9b$ d) $5a + 9b$ (1 mark)

2) What is the expression $7a - 4b + 6a - 3b$ when it is fully simplified?
  a) $7b - a$ b) $13a + 7b$ c) $a - 7b$ d) $13a - 7b$ (1 mark)

3) What is the expression $3(2x - 1)$ when it is multiplied out?
  a) $6x - 3$ b) $6x - 1$ c) $2x - 3$ d) $6x + 3$ (1 mark)

4) Factorise fully the expression $25x + 15$
  a) $5(5x + 15)$ b) $25(x + 15)$ c) $5(5x + 3)$ d) $5(5x)$ (1 mark)

5) What is the expression $5(n - 3)$ when it is multiplied out?
  a) $5n - 3$ b) $5n + 15$ c) $3n - 5$ d) $5n - 15$ (1 mark)

Score / 5

Short-answer questions

Answer all parts of each question.

1) Decide whether these simplified expressions are **true** or **false**. [U2|U3]
  a) $3a - 2b + 5a + b = 8a - b$ (1 mark)
  b) $6ay - 3ay^2 + 2ay^2 - 4ay = 2ay - ay^2$ (1 mark)
  c) $3ab + 2a^2b - a^2b + 4ba = a^2b + 12a^2 + b^2$ (1 mark)

2) Some expressions are written on cards. Choose an expression and copy it in each space to make each statement correct.

| $3n - 3$ | $8(n + 2)$ | $n^2 + 3n$ | $n^2 + 2$ | $5(n + 3)$ | $3n - 9$ |

  a) $3(n - 3) = $ _____   b) $5n + 15 = $ _____
  c) $n(n + 3) = $ _____   d) $8n + 16 = $ _____   (4 marks)

3) Factorise the following expressions.
  a) $10n + 15$ _____   b) $24 - 36n$ _____
  c) $5 + 10n$ _____   d) $20 - 4n$ _____
  e) $6a^2 + 12a$ _____   (5 marks)

Score / 12

GCSE-style questions

Answer all parts of the questions. Show your workings (on a separate sheet of paper if necessary) and include the correct units in your answers.

1 Here is a table for a two-stage number machine. It multiplies by 4 and subtracts 2. Complete the missing numbers in the table.

× 4 − 2	
Input	Output
1	2
2	6
4	
6	
	34

(3 marks)

2 a) Simplify $t + t$ .... (1 mark)

b) Simplify $y^2 + y^2 + y^2$ .... (1 mark)

3 a) Simplify fully $7n - 4n + 3n$ .... (1 mark)

b) Simplify fully $3a \times 2b$ .... (1 mark)

4 a) Expand and simplify $6x - 2(x - 2)$

.... (2 marks)

b) i) Factorise $6a + 12$ .... (1 mark)

ii) Factorise completely $10a^2 - 15ab$ .... (2 marks)

5 Show that $n(n + 2) - 3(n - 1)$ simplifies to $n^2 - n + 3$

....

.... (3 marks)

6 a) Expand and simplify $2(3a - 1) - (a - 2)$

....

.... (2 marks)

b) Factorise fully the following expressions.

i) $3n - 12$ .... (1 mark)

ii) $8pq - 12p$ .... (1 mark)

Score / 19

How well did you do?

0–10 Try again 11–18 Getting there 19–28 Good work 29–36 Excellent!

For more information on this topic, see pages 48–49 of your Success Revision Guide.

Formulae

Multiple-choice questions

Choose just one answer, a, b, c or d. Circle your choice.

1 Rearrange the formula $a = b + 4c$ to make c the subject.

   a) $c = \frac{a+b}{4}$ ⭕   b) $c = a + 4b$ c) $c = \frac{a-b}{4}$ d) $c = 4b + a$ (1 mark)

2 Rearrange the formula $P = 5a + b$ to make a the subject.

   a) $a = \frac{P-b}{5}$ b) $a = \frac{P+b}{5}$ c) $a = 5P + b$ d) $a = 5P - b$ (1 mark)

3 If $a = \frac{b}{c}$ and $b = 12$ and $c = 4$, what is the value of a?

   a) 12   b) 4   c) 6   d) 3   (1 mark)

4 There are n books in a pile. Each book is 5cm thick. What is the formula for the total height, h, of the pile of books?

   a) $5n$ b) $h = 5n$ c) $h = \frac{n}{5}$ d) $h = \frac{5}{n}$ (1 mark)

5 If $m = \sqrt{\frac{r^2 p}{4}}$ and $r = 3$ and $p = 6$, what is the positive value of m to 1 decimal place?

   a) 13.5   b) 182.3   c) 3.7   d) 3   (1 mark)

Score / 5

Short-answer questions

Answer all parts of each question.

1 Rearrange each of the formulae below to make b the subject.

   a) $p = 3b - 4$ (1 mark)

   b) $y = \frac{ab - 6}{4}$ (1 mark)

   c) $5(n + b) = 2b + 2$ (1 mark)

2 $F = ma$ is a formula. **True** or **false**?

                                                        (1 mark)

3 $a = \frac{b^2 + 2c}{4}$

   a) Calculate a if $b = 2$ and $c = 6$.   (1 mark)

   b) Calculate a if $b = 3$ and $c = -2$.   (1 mark)

   c) Calculate b if $a = 25$ and $c = 18$.   (1 mark)

4 John buys b books costing £6 each and m magazines costing 67 pence each. Write down a formula for the total cost (T) of the books and magazines.

   $T =$ (2 marks)

Score / 9

Algebra

46

GCSE-style questions

Answer all parts of the questions. Show your workings (on a separate sheet of paper if necessary) and include the correct units in your answers.

1 a) Using algebra, write in symbols the rule 'To find p, multiply n by 5 and then subtract 6.'

(1 mark)

b) Work out the value of p when $n = -2$.

(1 mark)

2 A shop sells white and brown bread. A loaf of white bread costs w pence and a loaf of brown bread costs b pence. James buys four loaves of white bread and five loaves of brown bread for his café. The total cost is C pence. Write down a formula for C in terms of w and b.

(3 marks)

3 Imran and Sophie use this rule to work out their pay:

> Pay = number of hours worked × amount paid per hour

a) Imran worked for 27 hours. He was paid £5.70 per hour. What was Imran's pay?

£............

(2 marks)

b) Sophie's pay was £192.20. She was paid £6.20 per hour. For how many hours did Sophie work?

.... hours (2 marks)

4 A person's body mass index (BMI), b, is calculated using the formula $b = \frac{m}{h^2}$ where m is the person's mass in kilograms and h is their height in metres.
A person is classed as overweight if their BMI is greater than 25. Peter has a height of 184cm and a mass of 89.5kg. Would Peter be classed as overweight? You must show working to justify your answer.

(3 marks)

5 The time for cooking a turkey is given by the formula:

> Cooking time in minutes = weight in kilograms × 40 + 35

a) A turkey weighs 7 kilograms. Find its cooking time.

.... minutes (2 marks)

b) A turkey takes 215 minutes to cook. Find its weight.

.... kilograms (3 marks)

Score / 17

How well did you do?

| 0–6 Try again | 7–15 Getting there | 16–20 Good work | 21–31 Excellent! |

For more information on this topic, see pages 50–51 of your Success Revision Guide.

Equations 1

Multiple-choice questions

Choose just one answer, a, b, c or d. Circle your choice.

1 Solve the equation $4n - 2 = 10$ U2 U3

     a) $n = 4$ b) $n = 2$ c) $n = 3$ d) $n = 3.5$ (1 mark)

2 Solve the equation $\frac{n}{2} + 4 = 2$

     a) $n = -4$ b) $n = 4$ c) $n = 12$ d) $n = -12$ (1 mark)

3 Solve the equation $4(x + 3) = 16$

     a) $x = 9$ b) $x = 7$ c) $x = 4$ d) $x = 1$ (1 mark)

4 Solve the equation $4(n + 2) = 8(n - 3)$

     a) $n = 16$ b) $n = 8$ c) $n = 4$ d) $n = 12$ (1 mark)

5 Solve the equation $10 - 6n = 4n - 5$

     a) $n = 2$ b) $n = -2$ c) $n = 1.5$ d) $n = -1.5$ (1 mark)

Score   / 5

Short-answer questions

Answer all parts of each question.

1 Solve the following equations.   U2 U3

     a) $n - 3 = 6$ b) $n + 10 = 12$

     c) $3n - 1 = 5$ d) $5 - n = 12$

     e) $\frac{n}{6} = 3$ f) $5n + 1 = 6$ (6 marks)

2 Reece thinks of a number. He adds 4 to the number. He then multiplies the result by 5. His answer is 25. What number did Reece think of?

     (2 marks)

3 Solve the following equations.

     a) $5n = 25$ b) $\frac{100}{n} = 25$

     c) $2n - 4 = 10$ d) $3 - 2n = 14$

     e) $\frac{n}{5} + 2 = 7$ f) $4 - \frac{n}{2} = 2$ (6 marks)

4 Solve the following equations.

     a) $12n + 5 = 3n + 32$ b) $5n - 4 = 3n + 6$

     c) $5(n + 1) = 25$ d) $4(n - 2) = 3(n + 2)$ (4 marks)

Score   / 18

Algebra

48

Success

AQA
GCSE Mathematics
Foundation
Workbook Answers

Answers

Statistics and probability

Page 6 – Collecting data

Multiple-choice questions
1. b
2. d
3. a
4. b

Short-answer questions
1.

Type of book	Tally	Frequency

2. The tick boxes overlap. Which box would somebody who did 2 hours of homework tick? The survey also needs to allow for students who do more than 4 hours of homework.
How much time do you spend, to the nearest hour, doing homework each night?

0 – 1 hours	2 – 3 hours	4 – 5 hours	6 or more hours

3. She is asking only men and not both men and women. She is also asking men who are interested in football as they are going to a football match, so her results will be biased.

GCSE-style questions
1.

Make of vehicle	Tally	Frequency

2. The question is too vague – what is meant by a 'healthy diet'? Also, the tick boxes are too vague – how often is 'sometimes'?
3. From the list below, tick your favourite chocolate bar.
   Mars ☐
   Twix ☐
   Toblerone ☐
   Galaxy ☐
   Bounty ☐
   Snickers ☐
   Other _____
4. The key to this question is to break it into subgroups.
   • On average, how many hours per school day do you watch television?
   0 up to 1 hour ☐
   1 up to 2 hours ☐
   2 up to 3 hours ☐
   3 up to 4 hours ☐
   More than 4 hours ☐
   • On average, how many hours at the weekend do you watch television?
   0 up to 2 hours ☐
   2 up to 4 hours ☐
   4 up to 6 hours ☐
   6 up to 8 hours ☐
   More than 8 hours ☐

Page 8 – Representing data

Multiple-choice questions
1. d
2. c
3. a
4. b

Short-answer questions
1. [Pie chart: Salt & Vinegar 150°, Beef 105°, Cheese & Onion, Smoky Bacon 15°]

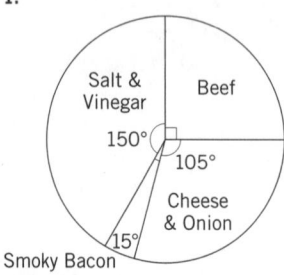

2.

Day	1	2	3	4	5	6	7
Hours of sunshine	3	4	1.5	1	1	3	1.5

GCSE-style questions
1. a) i) 14
      ii) 17
   b)

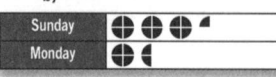

| Sunday | ●●●◔ |
| Monday | ●◐ |

2. a) Thursday
   b) Wednesday
   c) 32
   d) Jackie is not right. She sells 73 packets of cheese-flavour crisps whereas she sells 76 packets of salt and vinegar.

3. A frequency polygon showing students' heights [graph with Height (cm) on x-axis 130-160, Frequency on y-axis]

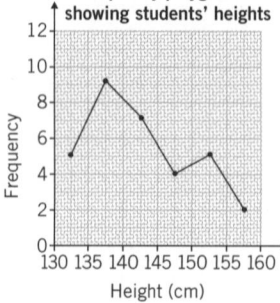

Page 10 – Scatter graphs & correlation

Multiple-choice questions
1. c
2. a
3. b

Short-answer questions
1. a) Positive correlation
   b) Negative correlation
   c) Positive correlation
   d) No correlation
2. a) Positive correlation
   b) [Scatter graph: Physics (%) vs Mathematics (%) with line of best fit]
   c) Approximately 74%

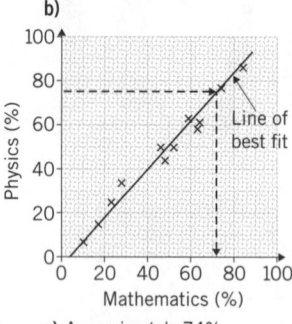

GCSE-style questions
1. a) [Scatter graph: Number of hours of sleep vs Age (in years) with line of best fit]
   b) Negative correlation – the younger the child, the more hours of sleep they needed.
   c) See line of best fit on graph above.
   d) A 4-year-old child has approximately 14 hours of sleep.
   e) This only gives an estimate as it follows the trend of the data. Similarly, if you continued the line it would assume that you may eventually need no hours sleep at a certain age, which is not the case.
   f) The child psychologist is not correct. From the data, 5-year-old children have approximately 13 hours of sleep.

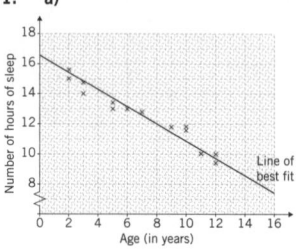

Page 12 – Averages 1

Multiple-choice questions
1. c
2. b
3. d

Short-answer questions
1. a) False
   b) True
   c) False
   d) True

2. a) Mean = 141.35
   b) The manufacturer is justified in making this claim because the mean is just over 141, and the mode and median are also approximately 141.
3. $x = 17$

GCSE-style questions
1. a) 11.5
   b) 8
   c) 10.6 (1 d.p.)
2. 7, 7, 13
3. 4.65
4. 81
5. £440

Page 14 – Averages 2

Multiple-choice questions
1. c
2. b
3. a
4. a

Short-answer questions
1. 21.5mm
2. a) Mode 47
   b) Median 35
   c) Range 40

GCSE-style questions
1. 1 | 2 4 9 5 7 5 8 8
   2 | 2 7 3 5 7 7
   3 | 1 6 5 2 8
   4 | 1
   Reordering gives:
   1 | 2 4 5 5 7 8 8 9
   2 | 2 3 5 7 7 7
   3 | 1 2 5 6 8
   4 | 1
   Key: 1 | 2 means 12 minutes

2. a) £31.80
   b) This is only an estimate because the midpoints of the class intervals have been used.
   c) $30 \leqslant x < 40$
   d) Although the modal class interval is $10 \leqslant x < 20$, since the mean is £31.80 and the median class interval is $30 \leqslant x < 40$, Edward's claim is not correct because the other averages indicate that the average amount spent is between £30 and £40.

Page 16 – Probability 1

Multiple-choice questions
1. c
2. d
3. c
4. b
5. a

1

Short-answer questions
1. a) $\frac{2}{11}$
    b) $\frac{2}{11}$
    c) $\frac{3}{11}$
    d) 0
2. 0.4
3. a) True
    b) False
    c) False
4. 100 students

GCSE-style questions
1.

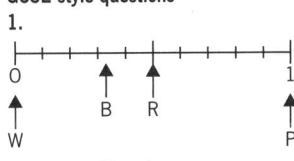

```
 0———————————1
   ↑   ↑   ↑
   B   R
 ↑         ↑
 W         P
```

2. a) i) $\frac{5}{20} = \frac{1}{4}$
       ii) $\frac{7}{20}$
    b) $\frac{16}{20} = \frac{4}{5}$
3. a) i) 0.35
       ii) 0
    b) There cannot be 12 counters in the bag because 0.1 × 12 = 1.2, hence not a whole number of counters.
    c) 50 times

Page 18 – Probability 2

Multiple-choice questions
1. c
2. a
3. a
4. d

Short-answer questions
1. a)

	1	2	3	3
1	2	3	4	4
2	3	4	5	5
3	4	5	6	6
6	7	8	9	9

   b) i) $\frac{4}{16} = \frac{1}{4}$
      ii) $\frac{2}{16} = \frac{1}{8}$
      iii) 0
2. HO, HT, CO, CT, BO, BT
    (H = Ham; C = Cheese; B = Beef; O = Orange; T = Tea)

GCSE-style questions
1. a) $\frac{6}{36} = \frac{1}{6}$
    b) $\frac{4}{36} = \frac{1}{9}$
2. a)

	Under 13 years old	13 years and over	Total
Boys	15	27	42
Girls	12	21	33
Total	27	48	75

    b) $\frac{27}{75} = \frac{9}{25}$
3. a) SS, SF, TS, TF, AS, AF
    b) $\frac{1}{6}$

Number

Page 20 – Number revision

Multiple-choice questions
1. d
2. c
3. a
4. c
5. d

Short-answer questions
1. a) 3 tens
    b) 3 thousands
    c) 3 hundred thousands
2. a) Six hundred and two
    b) Five thousand seven hundred and twenty-nine
3. a) 436
    b) 6 000 405
4. a) 6, 47, 75, 93, 102, 827, 1436
    b) 159, 729, 3692, 4138, 4207, 4879

GCSE-style questions
1. a) 1700
    b) 170 000
2. a) 16 431
    b) 3 ten thousands = 30 000
    c) 2358
3. a) One thousand and sixty-one pounds
    b) £2140
4. a) i) 18, 61, 72, 104, 130
       ii) 18, 19, 62, 397, 407
    b) Three (9, 12 and 15)

Page 22 – Numbers

Multiple-choice questions
1. d
2. b
3. c
4. a
5. b

Short-answer questions
1. a) True
    b) False
    c) False
    d) False
2. a) ±2
    b) ±10
    c) 64
    d) 2
    e) -5
    f) 169
3. $72 = 2^3 × 3^2$
4. $a = 2, b = 2$
5. 60
6. 8
7. True

GCSE-style questions
1. a) 1, 9, 16, 25
    b) 1, 6, 12, 24
    c) 11, 17
2. a) i) $56 = 2 × 2 × 2 × 7$ (or $2^3 × 7$)
       ii) $60 = 2 × 2 × 3 × 5$ (or $2^2 × 3 × 5$)
    b) HCF = 4
    c) LCM = 840
3. $360 = 2^3 × 3^2 × 5$
    Hence $a = 3, b = 2, c = 1$
4. a) 12m
    b) £240
5. Even number

Page 24 – Positive & negative numbers

Multiple-choice questions
1. a
2. d
3. b
4. b
5. c

Short-answer questions
1. a) -7 and 5
    b) -7 and -3
    c) 5 and -3
2. -3 × 4 → 10
    12 ÷ (-2) → -1
    -4 – (-3) → -12
    -5 × (-2) → 4
    -20 ÷ (-5) → -6
    (matching lines)
3. a) 10
    b) -10
    c) 14

GCSE-style questions
1. a) 18 degrees
    b) i) 17°C
       ii) 19 degrees
2. a) 12 degrees
    b) 4°C
    c) -11°C
3. -13, -5, -4, -2, 0, 1, 8, 9
4. $w = -2\ \ x = -5\ \ y = -11$

Page 26 – Working with numbers

Multiple-choice questions
1. b
2. c
3. a
4. b
5. d

Short-answer questions
1. 6 × 10 → 2400
    70 × 1000 → 70 000
    240 ÷ 100 → 60
    600 ÷ 1000 → 2.4
    80 × 30 → 0.6
2. a) 421
    b) 365
    c) 15 888
    d) 832
3. a) 7254
    b) 7632
    c) 17
    d) 48
4. £8804

GCSE-style questions
1. a)

Item	Cost	Number bought	Total cost
Bread	79p	4	£3.16
Milk	72p	2	£1.44
Cleaning fluid	£2.76	2	£5.52

    b) £5.12
2. a) 2976 sheets of paper
    b) 6 reams of paper
3. a) £5.15
    b) 12 fibre-tip pens
4. 33 students

Page 28 – Fractions

Multiple-choice questions
1. a
2. b
3. c
4. a
5. c

Short-answer questions
1. a) $\frac{3}{10}, \frac{1}{2}, \frac{2}{3}, \frac{3}{4}, \frac{4}{5}$
    b) $\frac{1}{9}, \frac{1}{3}, \frac{2}{5}, \frac{5}{8}, \frac{3}{4}$
2. a) True
    b) False
3. a) $\frac{5}{9}$
    b) $\frac{17}{44}$
    c) $\frac{3}{14}$
    d) 3
    e) $\frac{2}{3}$
    f) $\frac{5}{9}$
    g) $\frac{7}{8}$
    h) $\frac{11}{12}$
4. a) $2\frac{1}{2}$
    b) $1\frac{2}{3}$
    c) $4\frac{1}{2}$
    d) $1\frac{1}{11}$
5. a) $\frac{4}{22}$
    b) $\frac{28}{49}$
    c) $\frac{1}{4}$
    d) $\frac{36}{51}$

GCSE-style questions
1. 28 students
2. 7 weeks
3. 27
4. a) $1\frac{7}{15}$
    b) $\frac{16}{33}$
    c) $\frac{8}{63}$
    d) $\frac{3}{4}$
5. $\frac{7}{15}$
6. $\frac{1}{4} + \frac{1}{6} = \frac{6}{24} + \frac{4}{24} = \frac{10}{24}$
    $\frac{10}{24} × \frac{1}{2} = \frac{5}{24}$, which is not $\frac{1}{5}$
7. $115\frac{1}{2}$ kg

Page 30 – Decimals

Multiple-choice questions
1. c
2. b
3. c
4. b
5. d

Short-answer questions
1. a) Molly
   b) 1.201 seconds
   c) 0.002 seconds
2. a) False
   b) True
   c) True
3. a) 16
   b) 100
   c) 2000
   d) 0.1
   e) 24
   f) 0.01

GCSE-style questions
1. a) Ryan: £3.40
      Dom: £2.03
   b) The total is £5.43. Ryan has added 3 and 4 together to get the 70 pence. He has also not written the money to 2 decimal places.
2. a) 6.14, 6.141, 7.208, 7.29, 7.42
   b) 1.28
   c) 34.199
   d) i) 7.21
      ii) 6.14
3. a) $\frac{313}{1000}$
   b) 0.55
4. a) 0.01
   b) 0.1
   c) 0.001
5. £104.88

Page 32 – Percentages 1

Multiple-choice questions
1. c
2. c
3. d
4. d
5. a

Short-answer questions
1. £26 265
2. £102
3. 77%
4. £11.98
5. 40%
6. 10% of 30 — 16
   40% of 40 — 5
   5% of 15 — 3
   25% of 20 — 0.75

GCSE-style questions
1. Test 1, since 70 out of 90 is approximately 78% compared to 36 out of 48, which is 75%.
2. £4307.55
3. 12% reduction
4. £30.63
5. £340

Page 34 – Percentages 2

Multiple-choice questions
1. c
2. b
3. a

Short-answer questions
1. £168.03
2. £75.60
3. £7920
4. £560
5. 25%
6. 20%

GCSE-style questions
1. 1.61m
2. £119.36
3. £1000
4. £160
5. £3400
6. £8480
7. £255

Page 36 – Fractions, decimals & percentages

Multiple-choice questions
1. c
2. b
3. d
4. d
5. a

Short-answer questions
1.

Fraction	Decimal	Percentage
$\frac{2}{5}$	0.4	40%
$\frac{1}{20}$	0.05	5%
$\frac{1}{3}$	0.$\dot{3}$	33.$\dot{3}$%
$\frac{1}{25}$	0.04	4%
$\frac{1}{4}$	0.25	25%
$\frac{1}{8}$	0.125	12.5%

2. 30%, $\frac{1}{3}$, 0.37, $\frac{3}{8}$, $\frac{1}{2}$, 0.62, 92%
3. Rosebushes is cheaper because $\frac{1}{4}$ = 25%, which is greater than the reduction at Gardens Are Us.

GCSE-style questions
1. She should choose Sheila's Bargains since the TV costs £217.38. The TV is £14.62 cheaper than the most expensive TV at Gita's TV Shop.
2. $\frac{1}{8}$, 25%, 0.27, $\frac{1}{3}$, $\frac{2}{5}$, 0.571, 72%
3. Both will give the same answer because increasing by 20% is the same as multiplying by 1.2. Finding 10% then doubling it gives 20%, which when you add it to 40 is the same as increasing £40 by 20%.

Page 38 – Approximating & using a calculator

Multiple-choice questions
1. d
2. b
3. d
4. c
5. c

Short-answer questions
1. a) True
   b) False
   c) False
   d) True
2. a) 365.4
   b) 10.18402…
   c) 6324.361418
3. a) 100
   b) 90
4. £120

GCSE-style questions
1. 7.085523608
2. a) 5.937102473
   b) $\frac{30 \times 6}{40 - 10} = \frac{180}{30} = 6$
3. a) -856.859 65
   b) -900
4. a) 30 and 80
   b) 2400
   c) 49
5. $\frac{5}{2}$

Page 40 – Ratio

Multiple-choice questions
1. c
2. d
3. d
4. b
5. c

Short-answer questions
1. a) 1 : 3
   b) 1 : 4
   c) 1 : 3
2. 1200ml
3. 4.5 days
4. £666.06
5. a) £10.25
   b) 48g
6. £40 000

GCSE-style questions
1. Butter: 125g
   Sugar: 100g
   Eggs: 5
   Flour: 112.5g
   Milk: 37.5ml
2. 6 days
3. £10.14
4. Vicky: £6400
   Tracy: £8000
5. £4800
6. The 1-litre bottle gives the better value for money: 25cl × 4 = 1 litre, so the cost of four 25cl bottles would be £2.44, while the 1-litre bottle costs £1.52

Page 42 – Indices

Multiple-choice questions
1. a
2. b
3. d
4. d
5. a

Short-answer questions
1. a) 64
   b) 32
   c) 81
2. a) False
   b) False
   c) True
   d) True
   e) False
   f) True
3. a) $6a^2$
   b) $3m^2$
   c) $20a^3b^5$
   d) n^{16}
   e) a^{11}
   f) $2a^7$
   g) $12a^{11}$
   h) $3b^2$

4. a) n = 6
   b) n = 14
   c) n = 1
   d) n = 16

GCSE-style questions
1. Michelle is wrong since she has multiplied the indices instead of adding them. $m^3 \times m^2 = m^5$
2. a) i) 16
      ii) 27
   b) 9^5
3. a) p^7
   b) n^3
   c) a^6
   d) $4ab$
   e) $10n^{11}$
4. a) 3
   b) 25
   c) 648
5. a) i) 8
      ii) 36
      iii) 32
   b) 5^4
6. a) $6a^5$
   b) $3a$
   c) $\frac{1}{4b^2}$
   d) $8x^6$
7. a) i) 49
      ii) 243
      iii) 16
   b) 3^8

Algebra

Page 44 – Algebra

Multiple-choice questions
1. c
2. d
3. a
4. c
5. d

Short-answer questions
1. a) True
   b) True
   c) False
2. a) $3n - 9$
   b) $5(n + 3)$
   c) $n^2 + 3n$
   d) $8(n + 2)$
3. a) $5(2n + 3)$
   b) $12(2 - 3n)$
   c) $5(1 + 2n)$
   d) $4(5 - n)$
   e) $6a(a + 2)$

GCSE-style questions
1.

× 4 − 2	
Input	Output
1	2
2	6
4	14
6	22
9	34

2. a) $2t$
   b) $3y^2$
3. a) $6n$
   b) $6ab$
4. a) $4x + 4$
   b) i) $6(a + 2)$
      ii) $5a(2a - 3b)$

5. $n(n + 2) - 3(n - 1)$
   $= n^2 + 2n - 3n + 3$
   $= n^2 - n + 3$
6. a) $2(3a - 1) - (a - 2)$
      $= 6a - 2 - a + 2$
      $= 5a$
   b) i) $3(n - 4)$
      ii) $4p(2q - 3)$

Page 46 – Formulae

Multiple-choice questions
1. c
2. a
3. d
4. b
5. c

Short-answer questions
1. a) $b = \frac{p + 4}{3}$
   b) $b = \frac{4y + 6}{a}$
   c) $b = \frac{2 - 5n}{3}$
2. True
3. a) 4
   b) $\frac{5}{4}$ or 1.25
   c) ±8
4. $T = 6b + 0.67m$ or $T = 600b + 67m$

GCSE-style questions
1. a) $p = 5n - 6$
   b) $p = -16$
2. $C = 4w + 5b$
3. a) £153.90
   b) 31 hours
4. Peter's BMI $= \frac{89.5}{1.84^2} = 26.4$
   Peter would be classed as overweight.
5. a) 315 minutes
   b) 4.5kg

Page 48 – Equations 1

Multiple-choice questions
1. c
2. a
3. d
4. b
5. c

Short-answer questions
1. a) $n = 9$
   b) $n = 2$
   c) $n = 2$
   d) $n = -7$
   e) $n = 18$
   f) $n = 1$
2. 1
3. a) $n = 5$
   b) $n = 4$
   c) $n = 7$
   d) $n = -5.5$
   e) $n = 25$
   f) $n = 4$
4. a) $n = 3$
   b) $n = 5$
   c) $n = 4$
   d) $n = 14$

GCSE-style questions
1. a) $n = 4$
   b) $n = 3$
   c) $n = 5$
   d) $n = 14$
2. a) $m = 3$
   b) $p = \frac{6}{10}$ or $p = \frac{3}{5}$ or $p = 0.6$
   c) $x = 6$
   d) $x = 6$
3. $x = \frac{9}{5} = 1\frac{4}{5}$
4. a) 6
   b) $x = 1$

Page 50 – Equations 2 & inequalities

Multiple-choice questions
1. c
2. c
3. c
4. d
5. c

Short-answer questions
1. a) $x < 2$
   b) $x \geq 6$
   c) $1 \leq x \leq 4$
   d) $\frac{1}{3} \leq x \leq 2$
2. $2n + (n + 30°) + (n - 10°) = 180°$
   $4n + 20° = 180°$
   $n = 40°$
3. $t = 5.6$
   $t = -3.6$
   (You must show the full trial and improvement method in order to get full marks.)

GCSE-style questions
1. a) -3, -2, -1, 0, 1, 2
   b) $p \leq 2$
2. a) $9x + 12$
   b) $x = 3$; shortest side = 8cm
3. $x = 2.7$ (You must show the full trial and improvement method in order to get full marks)
4. $x = 2.8$ (You must show the full trial and improvement method in order to get full marks)

Page 52 – Number patterns & sequences

Multiple-choice questions
1. d
2. a
3. c
4. b

Short-answer questions
1. a) 10, 12
   b) 16, 19
   c) 121, 144
   d) 0.75, 0.375
2. a) Square numbers
   b) Powers of 10
   c) Cube numbers
3. a) 22
   b) $3n + 4$
4. a) False
   b) False
   c) True

GCSE-style questions
1. a) [dot pattern]
   b)

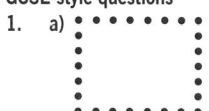

Pattern number	5	6
Number of dots	26	30

   c) 54
2. a) 28, 31
   b) Add 3 to the preceding term.
3. a) 2, 1, $\frac{1}{2}$
   b) $5n - 3$
4. $10 - 2n$

Page 54 – Straight-line graphs

Multiple-choice questions
1. b
2. d
3. d
4. c
5. a

Short-answer questions
1. Gradient = 4
2. a)

x	-2	-1	0	1	2
$y = 6 - x$	8	7	6	5	4

   b) [graph showing $y = 6 - x$ and part c)]
   c) i) See graph above.
      ii) 3
   d) (1, 5)

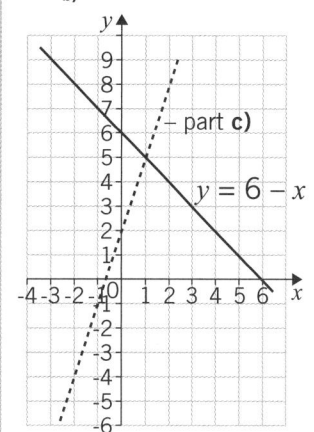

GCSE-style questions
1. a) P (-1, 2), Q (2, 3), R (3, -2)
   b) [graph of $y = x$]
2. a) [graph of $y = 2x - 2$ and $x + y = 4$]
   b) (2, 2)
3. $y = 2x \pm k$, where k is any number

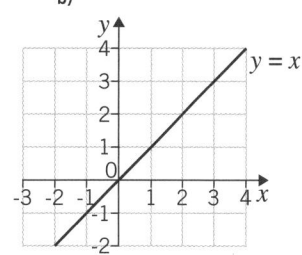

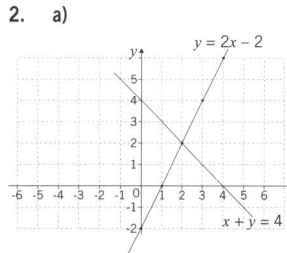

Page 56 – Quadratic graphs

Multiple-choice questions
1. b
2. d
3. c
4. d
5. b

Short-answer questions
1. a)

x	-2	-1	0	1	2	3
$y = x^2 - 2x - 2$	6	1	-2	-3	-2	1

   b) [graph of $y = x^2 - 2x - 2$]
   c) i) $y = -3$
      ii) $x = 2.7$, $x = -0.7$ (approx.)

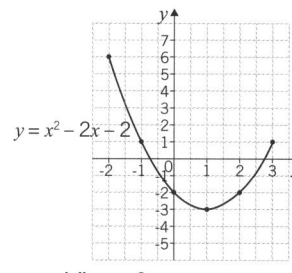

GCSE-style questions
1. a)

x	-3	-2	-1	0	1	2	3
$y = x^2 + 4$	13	8	5	4	5	8	13

   b) [graph of $y = x^2 + 4$ with $y = 13$ and $y = 10$]
   c) i) $x = 2.4$ or -2.4
      ii) $x = 3$ or -3

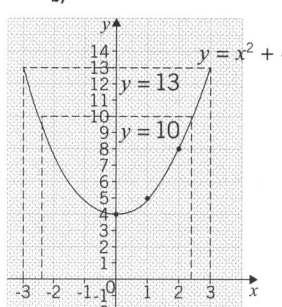

Page 58 – Interpreting graphs

Multiple-choice questions
1. c
2. d
3. a
4. d

Short-answer questions
1. Statement 1 matches graph C
   Statement 2 matches graph B
   Statement 3 matches graph A
2. Vase A matches graph 2
   Vase B matches graph 1
   Vase C matches graph 3

GCSE-style questions
1. a) $C = 30h + 40$
   b) i) £100
      ii) £190
   c) Mrs Robinson is correct since the standard charge is £40 and the rate is £30 per hour.
   £30 × 8 = £240
   £240 + £40 = £280

Geometry and measures

Page 60 – Shapes

Multiple-choice questions
1. d
2. d
3. c
4. a
5. b

Short-answer questions
1. a) True
   b) False
   c) False
   d) False
   e) True
2. a) Eight
   b) Six

GCSE-style questions
1. a) Quadrilateral
   b) Octagon
   c) Pentagon
   d) Triangle
2. Check on pages 66–67 of the Revision Guide.
3. (circle diagram: a) Diameter, b) Radius, c) Circumference, d) Arc)

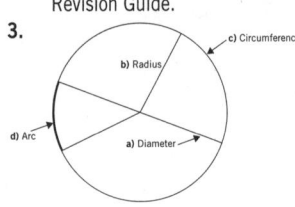

Page 62 – Solids

Multiple-choice questions
1. c
2. b
3. c
4. c
5. a

Short-answer questions
1. a) Cuboid
   b) Triangular prism
   c) Cylinder
2. (cuboid 2cm × 4cm × 3cm)
3. A, B and E

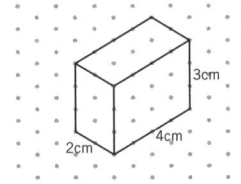

GCSE-style questions
1. (net with squares labelled 1, 5, 4, 2, 3, 6)
2. a) A possible answer: (net diagram)
   b) 9

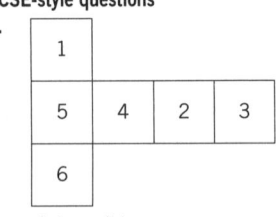

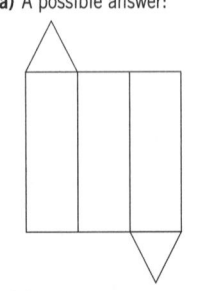

Page 64 – Angles

3. a) Plan   b) Front elevation 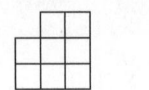
   c) Side elevation

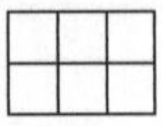

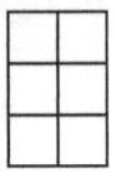

Multiple-choice questions
1. a
2. c
3. b
4. b
5. a

Short-answer questions
1. a) $n = 65°$
   b) $n = 63°$
   c) $n = 148°$
   d) $n = 68°$
   e) $n = 91°$
   f) $n = 60°$
   g) $n = 154°$
2. Any suitable tessellation, e.g.

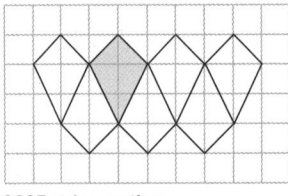

GCSE-style questions
1. 76° and 28° or 52° and 52°
2. a) i) $x = 18°$
      ii) If AB is vertical and BD is horizontal, angle ABE = 90° So, angle x must be 18°
   b) i) $y = 54°$
      ii) Triangle BCD is isosceles, so angles BDC and BCD are equal. Hence y must be 54°
   c) i) $z = 54°$
      ii) Angle z is an alternate angle with angle BDC since CF and BE are parallel.
3. a) Sum of interior angles in a hexagon $= (2n – 4) \times 90°$. Sum of angles in a hexagon is 720°. Angle $x = 105°$
   b) Sum of the exterior angles = 360°. Since there are six equal exterior angles, the size of one angle is $\frac{360°}{6} = 60°$.

Page 66 – Bearings & scale drawings

Multiple-choice questions
1. c
2. a
3. d
4. b

Short-answer questions
1. 10km
2. a) Your diagram should be drawn to scale. 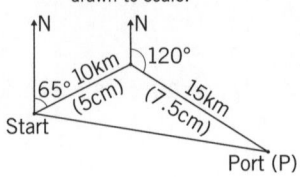
   (diagram: Start → 10km (5cm) at 65°, then 15km (7.5cm) at 120° to Port (P))
   b) 11.1cm = 22.2km
   c) 098° (±1°)
3. False, it is 240°

GCSE-style questions
1. a) 165m
   b) 210°
   c) Your diagram should be drawn to scale. 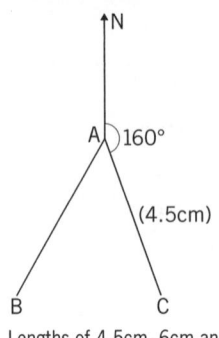
   (diagram: A at 160°, B and C, length 4.5cm)
2. Lengths of 4.5cm, 6cm and 7cm must be ±2mm.
   (triangle: 9m (4.5cm), 12m (6cm), 14m (7cm))

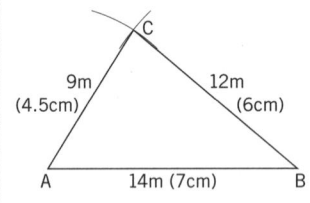

Page 68 – Transformations 1

Multiple-choice questions
1. c
2. d
3. d
4. b

Short-answer questions
1. (grid showing T, A, R, S)
2. a) True
   b) True
   c) False
   d) True

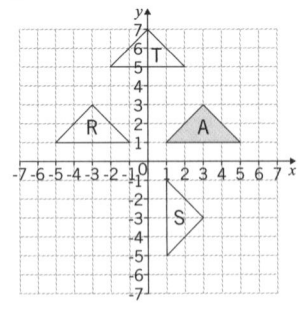

GCSE-style questions
1. a) Reflection in the x-axis
   b) Rotation 90° anticlockwise about (0, 0)

2. (grid showing R, T, Q, P)

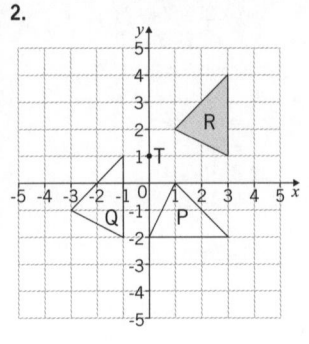

Page 70 – Transformations 2

Multiple-choice questions
1. b
2. b
3. a

Short-answer questions
1. (grid showing P, R, O)
2. a) Reflection in the y-axis
   b) Rotation 90° clockwise about (0, 0)
   c) Reflection in the line $y = x$

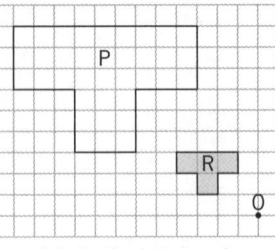

GCSE-style questions
1. a) (shape A on grid)
   b) $20cm^2$
2. a) (grid showing R, N, P)
   b) No, Daniel is not right. To be congruent they need to be the same size.

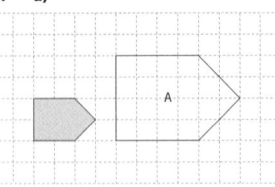

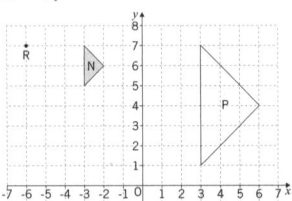

Page 72 – Symmetry & constructions

Multiple-choice questions
1. a
2. d
3. a
4. c
5. b

Short-answer questions
1. a) Any of these lines of symmetry.
   (hexagon with lines of symmetry)

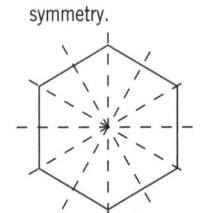

b)

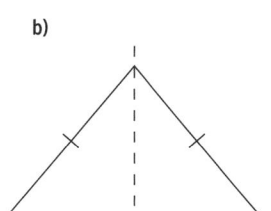

2. a) Construction arcs must be shown.

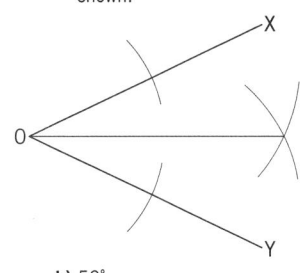

b) 50°
3. Your diagram should be drawn accurately and construction arcs must be shown.

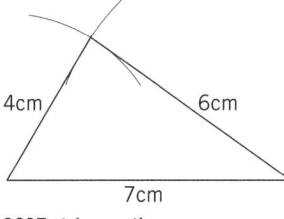

4cm, 6cm, 7cm

GCSE-style questions
1. a)

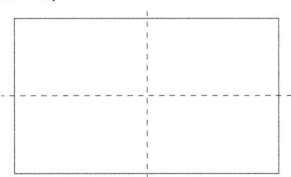

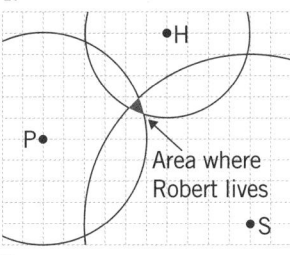

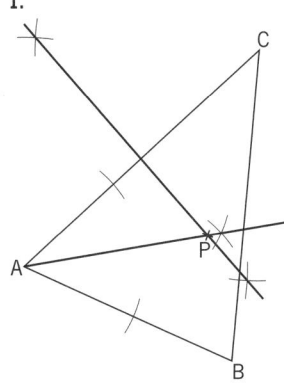

b) Order 2
2. a)

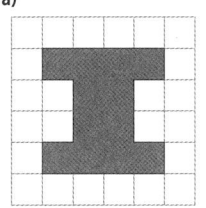

b) Order 2.
3. Construction arcs must be shown.

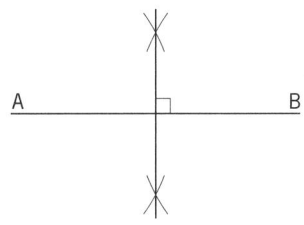

Page 74 – Loci & coordinates

Multiple-choice questions
1. c
2. a
3. d
4. b

Short-answer questions
1. [diagram showing area where Robert lives, with points P, H, S]
2. [diagram on grid]

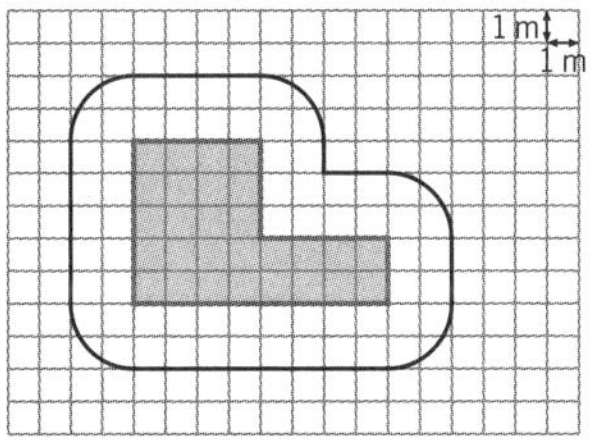

GCSE-style questions
1. [diagram with points A, B, C, P]
2. Vertex R (1, -1)

Page 76 – Measures & measurement 1

Multiple-choice questions
1. b
2. a
3. d
4. d
5. a

Short-answer questions
1.

12-hr	4:23pm	3:34pm	9:26pm	3:16pm	3:14am	9:38pm
24-hr	1623	1534	2126	1516	0314	2138

2. a) 10–15m
   b) About 260km
   c) 5ml
3. a) 6.7
   b) 9.4
   c) 12.75
   d) 7.34

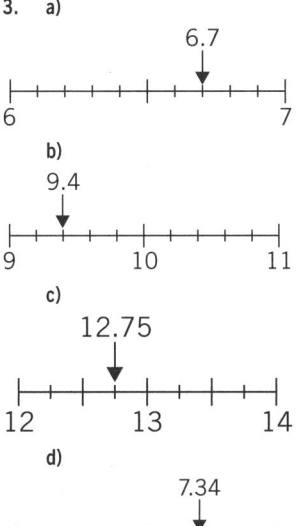

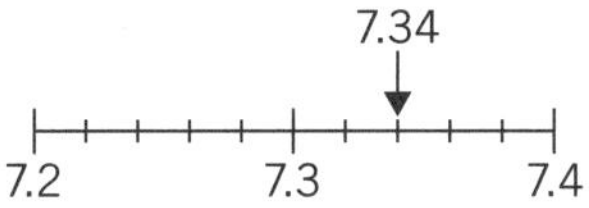

GCSE-style questions
1. a) 19.6
   b) 20
   c) 16
   d) 12.4
2. a) i) 31 minutes
      ii) 14 minutes
   b) 1806

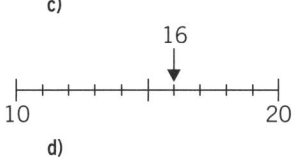

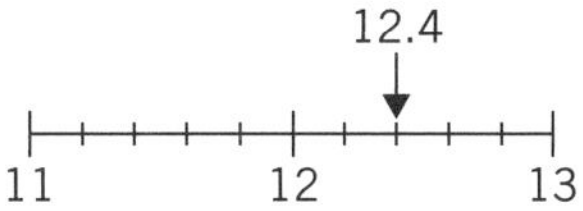

Page 78 – Measures & measurement 2

Multiple-choice questions
1. b
2. a
3. d
4. c
5. d

Short-answer questions
1. a) 8000m
   b) 3.25kg
   c) 7000kg
   d) 0.52m
   e) 2700ml
   f) 0.002 62km
2. 12.5 miles
3. 1.32 pounds
4. 60mph
5. 47.5 miles

GCSE-style questions
1. a) 17.6 pounds
   b) 48 kilometres
2. a) 1 hour 30 minutes = 90 minutes
   b) Average speed 5.1km/h
3. 111.5 grams
4. 4.5°C
5. 1 hour and 15 minutes.
6. $\frac{2400}{108} = 22.\dot{2}$m/s
   $\frac{22.\dot{2}}{4.47} = 4.97...$
   4.97×10mph $= 49.7$mph
   The car was not speeding through the roadworks.

Page 80 – Pythagoras' theorem

Multiple-choice questions
1. b
2. a
3. c
4. c

Short-answer questions
1. a) $n = 15$cm
   b) $n = 12.6$cm
   c) $n = 29.1$cm
   d) $n = 24.6$cm
2. Since
   $12^2 + 5^2 = 13^2$
   $144 + 25 = 169$
   the triangle must be right-angled for Pythagoras' theorem to be applied.
3. Both statements are true.
   Length of line = $\sqrt{6^2 + 3^2}$ = $\sqrt{45} = 6.7$ (1 d.p.)
   Midpoint = $\left(\frac{2+5}{2}\right), \left(\frac{5+11}{2}\right)$
   = (3.5, 8)

GCSE-style questions
1. 13.7m
2. 6.4cm
3. 48.6m
4. £13.52

Page 82 – Area of 2D shapes

Multiple-choice questions
1. c
2. d
3. b
4. d
5. b

Short-answer questions
1. a) False
   b) True
   c) False
2. 38.6cm
3. 84.21cm^2

GCSE-style questions
1. £33
2. 363.6cm^2 (1 d.p.)
3. 127cm (nearest cm)
4. £2170

Page 84 – Volume of 3D shapes

Multiple-choice questions
1. a
2. c
3. a
4. d

Short-answer questions
1. Emily is not correct. The correct volume is $345.6 \div 2 = 172.8$m^3
2. Volume = 170.2m^3
3. 1.85cm
4. 156cm^2

GCSE-style questions
1. 64cm^3
2. a) 672cm^3
   b) 0.000 672m^3
3. 5cm
4. £25.35
5. 1128cm^3

Answers

Answers

Published by Letts Educational Ltd.
An imprint of HarperCollins*Publishers*

Text © Fiona Mapp
Design and illustration © 2010 Letts Educational Ltd.

All rights reserved. No part of this publication may be reproduced, stored in a retrieval system, or transmitted, in any form or by any means, electronic, mechanical, photocopying, recording or otherwise, without the prior permission of Letts Educational Ltd.

GCSE-style questions

Answer all parts of the questions. Show your workings (on a separate sheet of paper if necessary) and include the correct units in your answers.

1 Solve these equations. (U2 U3)

   a) $3n = 12$ _____ (2 marks)

   b) $5n + 3 = 18$ _____ (3 marks)

   c) $3(n + 2) = 21$ _____ (3 marks)

   d) $\frac{n-2}{4} = 3$ _____ (2 marks)

2 Solve these equations.

   a) $5m - 3 = 12$ _____ (2 marks)

   b) $8p + 3 = 9 - 2p$ _____ (2 marks)

   c) $5(x - 1) = 3x + 7$ _____ (2 marks)

   d) $4 + x = 2(x - 1)$ _____ (2 marks)

3 Each expression in the wall is formed by adding the two supporting expressions from the row below.

For example:

```
        4x + 7
   3x + 5 | x + 2
```

$3x + 5 + x + 2 = 4x + 7$

Use the wall below to find the value of x.

```
           6
        2x + 5
   x + 1 | x + 4 | 2x - 12
```

(3 marks)

4 a) Amy thinks of a number. She adds 9 to the number. She then multiplies the result by 4. Her answer is 60. What number did Amy first think of?

_____

_____ (2 marks)

b) Solve $8 - 2x = 3x + 3$

_____

_____ (3 marks)

Score / 26

How well did you do?

0–19 Try again   20–28 Getting there   29–38 Good work   39–49 Excellent!

For more information on this topic, see pages 52–53 of your Success Revision Guide.

Equations 2 & inequalities

Multiple-choice questions

Choose just one answer, a, b, c or d. Circle your choice.

1) $-4 \leqslant y < 2$ and y is an integer. What are all the possible values of y?
   a) -4, -3, -2, -1, 0, 1, 2
   b) -3, -2, -1, 0, 1, 2
   c) -4, -3, -2, -1, 0, 1
   d) -3, -2, -1, 0, 1
   (1 mark)

2) $-6 \leqslant 2n < 2$ and n is an integer. What are all the possible values of n?
   a) -6, -5, -4, -3, -2, -1, 0, 1
   b) -3, -2, -1, 0, 1
   c) -3, -2, -1, 0
   d) -2, -1, 0, 1, 2
   (1 mark)

3) Solve the inequality $2x - 7 < 9$
   a) $x < 9$
   b) $x < 10$
   c) $x < 8$
   d) $x < 6.5$
   (1 mark)

4) Solve the inequality $3x + 1 < 19$
   a) $x < 3$
   b) $x < 7$
   c) $x < 5$
   d) $x < 6$
   (1 mark)

5) The equation $y^3 + 2y = 82$ has a solution between 4 and 5. By using a method of trial and improvement, find the solution to 1 decimal place.
   a) 3.9
   b) 4.1
   c) 4.2
   d) 4.3
   (1 mark)

Score / 5

Short-answer questions

Answer all parts of each question.

1) Solve the following inequalities.
   a) $5x + 2 < 12$ _____
   b) $\frac{x}{3} + 1 \geqslant 3$ _____
   c) $3 \leqslant 2x + 1 \leqslant 9$ _____
   d) $3 \leqslant 3x + 2 \leqslant 8$ _____
   (4 marks)

2) The angles in a triangle add up to 180°. Form an equation in n and solve it.

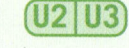

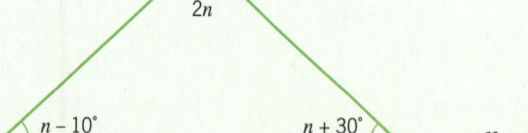

   (triangle with angles $2n$, $n - 10°$, $n + 30°$)

   $n = $ _____ (2 marks)

3) Use a method of trial and improvement to solve the following equation. Give your answer to 1 decimal place.

   $t^2 - 2t = 20$ $t = $ _____ or $t = $ _____
   (2 marks)

Score / 8

GCSE-style questions

Answer all parts of the questions. Show your workings (on a separate sheet of paper if necessary) and include the correct units in your answers.

1 n is an integer.

a) Write down the values of n that satisfy the inequality $-4 < n \leq 2$

(2 marks)

b) Solve the inequality $5p - 2 \leq 8$

(2 marks)

2 The lengths, in cm, of the sides of a triangle are $2x + 7$, $3x - 1$ and $4x + 6$.

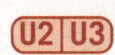

a) Write down, in terms of x, an expression for the perimeter of the triangle. Give your expression in its simplest form.

(2 marks)

b) The perimeter of the triangle is 39cm. Work out the length of the shortest side of the triangle.

(2 marks)

3 Use a method of trial and improvement to solve the equation $x^3 + 3x = 28$
Give your answer correct to 1 decimal place. You must show all your working.

$x = $ _____

(4 marks)

4 The equation $x^3 + 10x = 51$ has a solution between 2 and 3. Use a method of trial and improvement to find this solution. Give your answer correct to 1 decimal place. You must show all your working.

$x = $ _____

(4 marks)

Score / 16

How well did you do?

| 0–6 | Try again | 7–14 | Getting there | 15–22 | Good work | 23–29 | Excellent! |

For more information on this topic, see pages 54–57 of your Success Revision Guide.

Number patterns & sequences

Multiple-choice questions

Choose just one answer, a, b, c or d. Circle your choice.

1) What is the next number in the following sequence: 1, 4, 9, 16.
   a) 24   b) 49   c) 36   d) 25   (1 mark)

2) What is the *n*th term of a sequence whose first four terms are 5, 7, 9, 11?
   a) $2n + 3$ b) $2n - 3$ c) $n + 2$ d) $3 - 2n$ (1 mark)

3) If the *n*th term of a sequence is given by $4 - 3n$, what is the fifth term of this sequence?
   a) -8   b) -2   c) -11   d) -14   (1 mark)

4) What is the *n*th term of a sequence whose first four terms are 18, 16, 14, 12?
   a) $2n - 20$ b) $20 - 2n$ c) $n - 2$ d) $2n + 20$ (1 mark)

Score / 4

Short-answer questions

Answer all parts of each question.

1) Write down the next two terms in each of the sequences below.
   a) 2, 4, 6, 8, _____, _____
   b) 4, 7, 10, 13, _____, _____
   c) 49, 64, 81, 100, _____, _____
   d) 12, 6, 3, 1.5, _____, _____   (4 marks)

2) The cards below have some names of sequences.

   [Square numbers]   [Triangular numbers]
   [Powers of 10]   [Cube numbers]

   Match these sequences with the correct name.
   a) 16, 25, 36, 49 _____ (1 mark)
   b) 10, 100, 1000, 10 000 _____ (1 mark)
   c) 1, 8, 27, 64 _____ (1 mark)

3) Look at this sequence: 7, 10, 13, 16…
   a) What is the sixth number of this sequence? _____ (1 mark)
   b) Write down the *n*th term of this sequence. _____ (1 mark)

4) Decide whether the *n*th term given is **true** or **false** for each of these sequences.
   a) 1, 4, 7, 10, 13   *n*th term: $n + 3$ _____ (1 mark)
   b) 10, 6, 2, -2, -6   *n*th term: $10 - 4n$ _____ (1 mark)
   c) 1, 4, 7, 10   *n*th term: $3n - 2$ _____ (1 mark)

Score / 12

GCSE-style questions

Answer all parts of the questions. Show your workings (on a separate sheet of paper if necessary) and include the correct units in your answers.

1 Here are some patterns made up of dots.

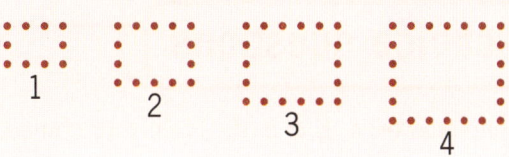

a) In the space below, draw pattern number 5.

(1 mark)

b) Complete the table.

Pattern number	1	2	3	4	5	6
Number of dots	10	14	18	22		

(1 mark)

c) How many dots are used in pattern number 12? .... (1 mark)

2 Here are the first four numbers of a simple sequence: 16, 19, 22, 25

a) Write down the next two numbers of the sequence. .... (2 marks)

b) Write down in words, the rule to continue this sequence.

.... (1 mark)

3 a) Here are the first five terms of a sequence: 64, 32, 16, 8, 4

Write down the next three terms in the sequence. ...., ..., ... (3 marks)

b) Here are the first five terms of a different sequence: 2, 7, 12, 17, 22
Find, in terms of n, an expression for the nth term for this sequence.

.... (2 marks)

4 Here are the first four numbers in a sequence: 8, 6, 4, 2
Write down, in terms of n, the nth term for this sequence.

.... (2 marks)

Score   / 13

How well did you do?

| 0–5 Try again | 6–10 Getting there | 11–20 Good work | 21–29 Excellent! |

For more information on this topic, see pages 56–57 of your Success Revision Guide.

Straight-line graphs

Multiple-choice questions

Choose just one answer, a, b, c or d. Circle your choice.

U2

1) Which point lies on the line $x = 2$?

   a) (1, 3)   b) (2, 3)   c) (3, 2)   d) (0, 2)   (1 mark)

2) Which point lies on the line $y = -3$?

   a) (-3, 5)   b) (5, -2)   c) (-2, 5)   d) (5, -3)   (1 mark)

3) What is the gradient of the line $y = 5x - 2$?

   a) -2   b) -5   c) 2   d) 5   (1 mark)

4) These graphs have been drawn: $y = 3x - 1$, $y = 6x + 1$, $y = 2x - 3$, $y = 5x - 3$
   Which graph is the steepest?

   a) $y = 3x - 1$ b) $y = 5x - 3$ c) $y = 6x + 1$ d) $y = 2x - 3$ (1 mark)

5) At what point does the graph $y = 3x - 4$ intercept the y-axis?

   a) (0, -4)   b) (0, 3)   c) (-4, 0)   d) (3, 0)   (1 mark)

Score / 5

Short-answer questions

Answer all parts of each question.

U2

1) What is the gradient of the line $y = 3 + 4x$? _____ (1 mark)

2) a) Complete the table of values for $y = 6 - x$.

x	-2	-1	0	1	2
$y = 6 - x$	___	___	6	___	4

(2 marks)

b) On the grid below, plot your values for x and y. Join your points with a straight line. (1 mark)

c) A second line goes through the coordinates (1, 5), (-2, -4) and (2, 8).

   i) Draw this line. (1 mark)

   ii) Write down the gradient of the line you have just drawn.

   _____ (2 marks)

d) What are the coordinates of the point where the two lines meet?

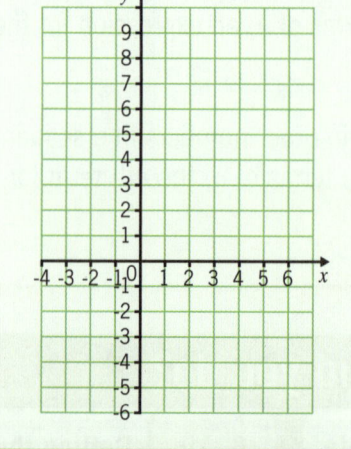

   _____ (1 mark)

Score / 8

54

GCSE-style questions

Answer all parts of the questions. Show your workings (on a separate sheet of paper if necessary) and include the correct units in your answers.

1 a) Triangle PQR is drawn on a grid.

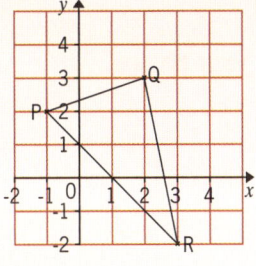

Write down the coordinates of P, Q and R.

P (........, ...)   Q (........, ...)   R (........, ...)   (3 marks)

b) On the grid draw the graph of $y = x$

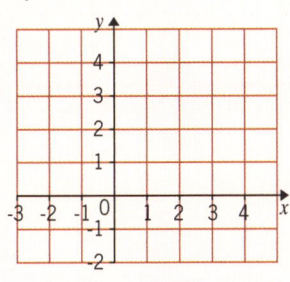

(2 marks)

2 The line with the equation $x + y = 4$ has been drawn on the grid.

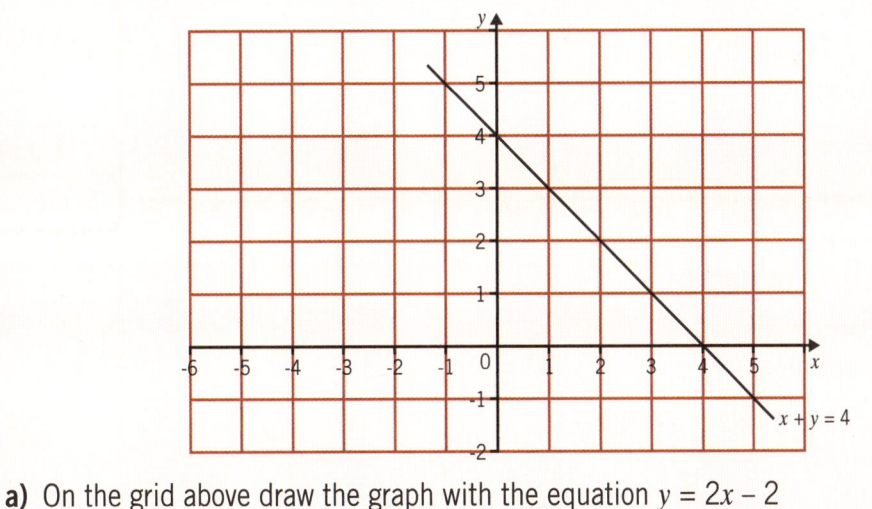

a) On the grid above draw the graph with the equation $y = 2x - 2$ (3 marks)

b) Write down the coordinates of the point of intersection of the two straight-line graphs.

(........, ...)   (1 mark)

3 Write down an equation of a straight line that is parallel to the line $y = 2x$.

....   (1 mark)

Score   / 10

How well did you do?

| 0–4 | Try again | 5–9 | Getting there | 10–16 | Good work | 17–23 | Excellent! |

For more information on this topic, see pages 58–59 of your Success Revision Guide.

Quadratic graphs

Multiple-choice questions

Choose just one answer, a, b, c or d. Circle your choice.

1 Which point lies on the graph $y = x^2 - 2$?

   a) (1, 1)   **b)** (4, 14)   **c)** (2, 4)   **d)** (0, 2)

U3

(1 mark)

2 On which of these curves do the coordinates (2, 5) lie?

   a) $y = x^2 - 4$ **b)** $y = 2x^2 + 3$ **c)** $y = x^2 - 6$ **d)** $y = 2x^2 - 3$

(1 mark)

Questions 3–5 refer to these diagrams:

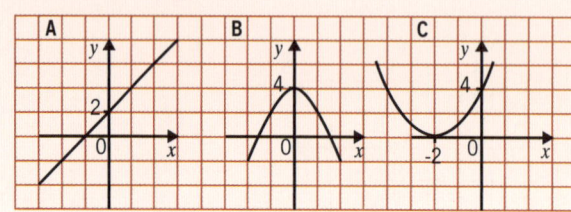

3 What is the equation of graph A?

   a) $y = 5 - 2x^2$ **b)** $y = x^2 + 4x + 4$ **c)** $y = x + 2$ **d)** $y = 4 - x^2$

(1 mark)

4 What is the equation of graph B?

   a) $y = 5 - 2x^2$ **b)** $y = x^2 + 4x + 4$ **c)** $y = x + 2$ **d)** $y = 4 - x^2$

(1 mark)

5 What is the equation of graph C?

   a) $y = 5 - 2x^2$ **b)** $y = x^2 + 4x + 4$ **c)** $y = x + 2$ **d)** $y = 4 - x^2$

(1 mark)

Score / 5

Short-answer questions

Answer all parts of each question.

1 a) Complete the table of values for $y = x^2 - 2x - 2$

x	-2	-1	0	1	2	3
$y = x^2 - 2x - 2$			-2			1

U3

(2 marks)

b) On the grid below, draw the graph of $y = x^2 - 2x - 2$ (3 marks)

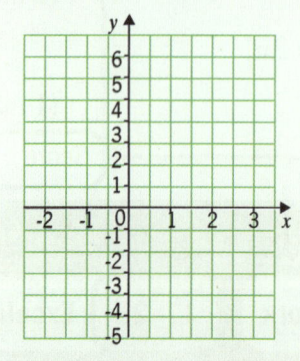

c) Use your graph to write down an estimate for...

   i) the minimum value of y

      $y =$ ....

(1 mark)

   ii) the solutions of the equation $x^2 - 2x - 2 = 0$

      $x =$ .... and $x =$ ....

(2 marks)

Score / 8

GCSE-style questions

Answer all parts of the questions. Show your workings (on a separate sheet of paper if necessary) and include the correct units in your answers.

1 a) Complete the table of values for the graph $y = x^2 + 4$

x	-3	-2	-1	0	1	2	3
$y = x^2 + 4$	13		5				13

(2 marks)

b) On the grid, draw the graph of $y = x^2 + 4$

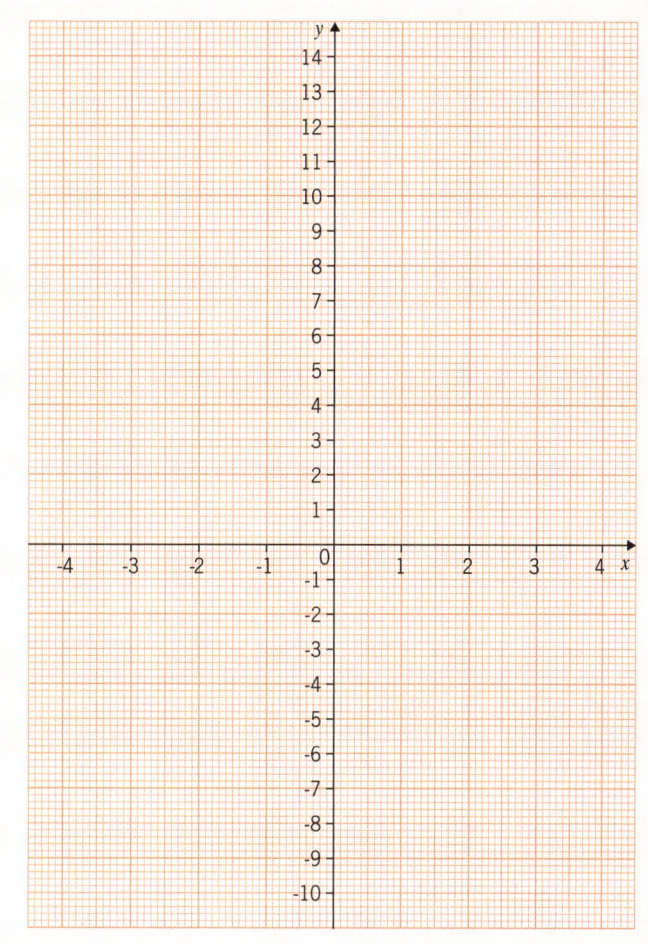

(2 marks)

c) Use your graph to find an estimate of...

  i) the solution of the equation $x^2 + 4 = 10$

  $x =$ ....

(1 mark)

  ii) the solution of the equation $x^2 + 4 = 13$

  $x =$ ....

(2 marks)

Score / 7

How well did you do?

0–4 Try again   5–9 Getting there   10–14 Good work   15–20 Excellent!

For more information on this topic, see pages 60–61 of your *Success Revision Guide*.

Interpreting graphs

Multiple-choice questions

Choose just one answer, a, b, c or d. Circle your choice.

1) If £1 = $1.48, how much would £10 be in American dollars?

   a) $0.148   b) $148   c) $14.80   d) $1480

   (1 mark)

Questions 2–4 refer to the graph opposite.
The graph shows Mrs Morgan's car journey.

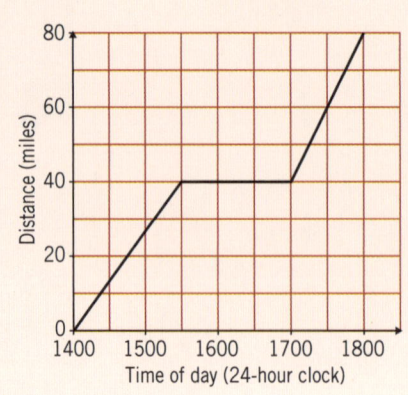

2) At what speed did Mrs Morgan travel for the first hour and a half?

   a) 25mph   b) 28mph   c) 30mph   d) 26.7mph

   (1 mark)

3) At what time did Mrs Morgan take a break from her car journey?

   a) 1530   b) 1600   c) 1400   d) 1500

   (1 mark)

4) At what speed did Mrs Morgan travel between 1700 and 1800 hours?

   a) 60mph   b) 80mph   c) 35mph   d) 40mph

   (1 mark)

Score / 4

Short-answer questions

Answer all parts of each question.

1) Match these graphs to the statements.

   1. A mobile phone company charges a standard fee plus a certain amount per call. Graph _____

   2. The price of shares dropped sharply, levelled off and then started rising. Graph _____

   3. Conversion between kilometres and miles. Graph _____

   (3 marks)

2) Water is poured into these odd-shaped vases at a constant rate. Match each vase to the correct graph.

   Vase A matches graph _____

   Vase B matches graph _____

   Vase C matches graph _____

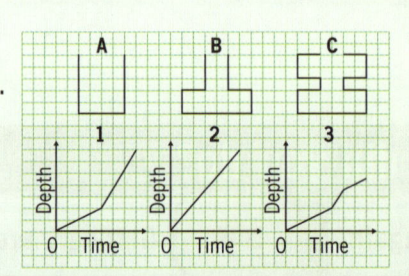

   (3 marks)

Score / 6

GCSE-style questions

Answer all parts of the questions. Show your workings (on a separate sheet of paper if necessary) and include the correct units in your answers.

1 The graph shows the cost, C (£), that a plumber charges for a number of hours, h.

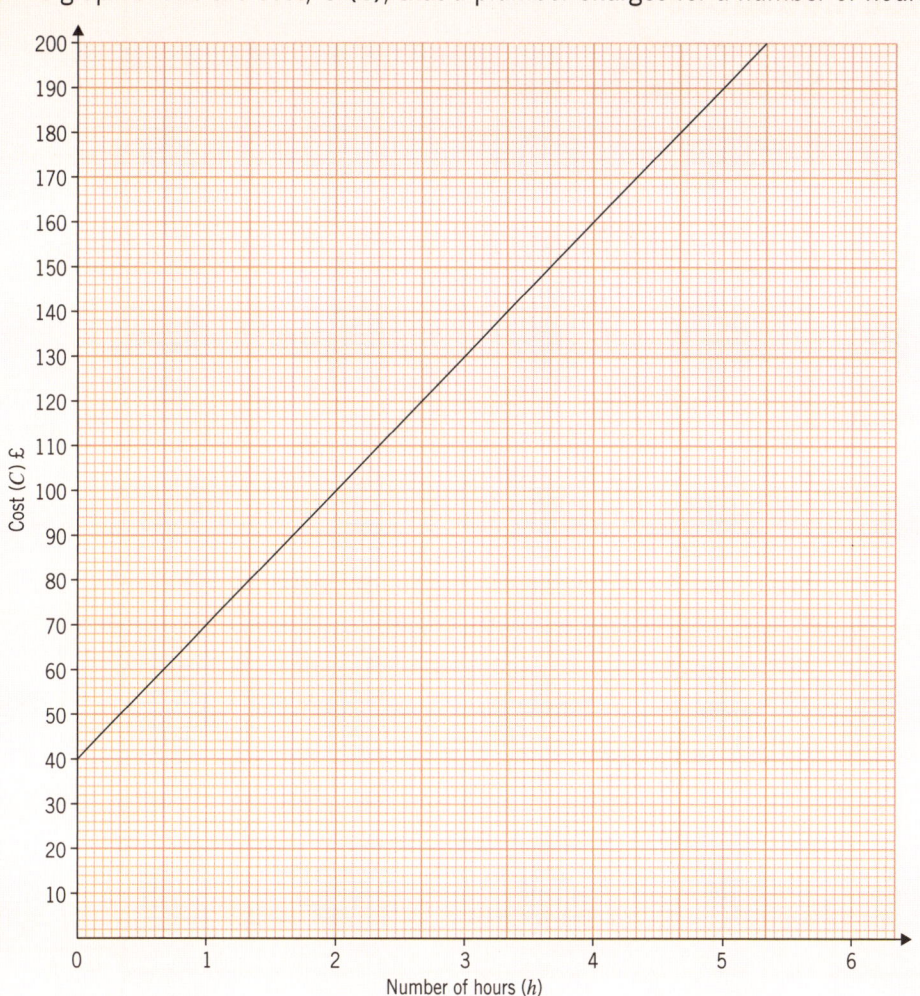

a) Circle the correct formula, connecting the cost (C) and the number of hours (h) the plumber works.

$C = 3h + 40$ $\qquad$ $C = 30h + 40$ $\qquad$ $C = 40h + 30$

(1 mark)

b) Work out the price the plumber will charge if he works for…

i) 2 hours .... (1 mark)

ii) 4 hours and 40 minutes (note all part hours are rounded to the nearest hour).

.... (1 mark)

c) If the plumber works for 8 hours, Mrs Robinson thinks she will be charged £280. Explain whether Mrs Robinson is correct.

.... (2 marks)

Score / 5

How well did you do?

0–4 Try again | 5–8 Getting there | 9–11 Good work | 12–15 Excellent!

For more information on this topic, see pages 62–63 of your *Success Revision Guide*.

Shapes

Multiple-choice questions

Choose just one answer, a, b, c or d. Circle your choice.

Questions 1–5 refer to the diagrams below.

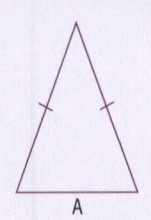

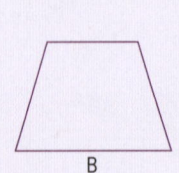

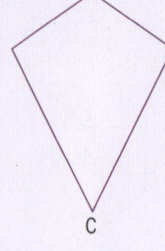

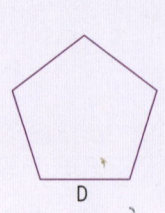

A   B   C   D

1 What is the name of shape B?   **U3**
   a) Triangle   b) Kite   c) Hexagon   d) Trapezium   (1 mark)

2 What is the name of shape D?
   a) Triangle   b) Parallelogram   c) Hexagon   d) Pentagon   (1 mark)

3 What special type of triangle is shape A?
   a) Equilateral   b) Scalene   c) Isosceles   d) Isolateral   (1 mark)

4 How many lines of symmetry does shape C have?
   a) 1   b) 2   c) 3   d) 4   (1 mark)

5 What is the name of shape C?
   a) Parallelogram   b) Kite   c) Trapezium   d) Rectangle   (1 mark)

Score   / 5

Short-answer questions

Answer all parts of each question.

1 These shapes are quadrilaterals. State whether each of these statements is **true** or **false**.   **U3**

A   B   C   D

   a) Shape B is a rectangle.   (1 mark)
   b) Shape D is a parallelogram.   (1 mark)
   c) Shape A has 2 lines of symmetry.   (1 mark)
   d) Shape B has rotational symmetry of order 4.   (1 mark)
   e) Shape C is a parallelogram.   (1 mark)

2 a) How many lines of symmetry does a regular octagon have?

    (1 mark)

   b) What is the order of rotational symmetry of a regular hexagon?   (1 mark)

Score   / 7

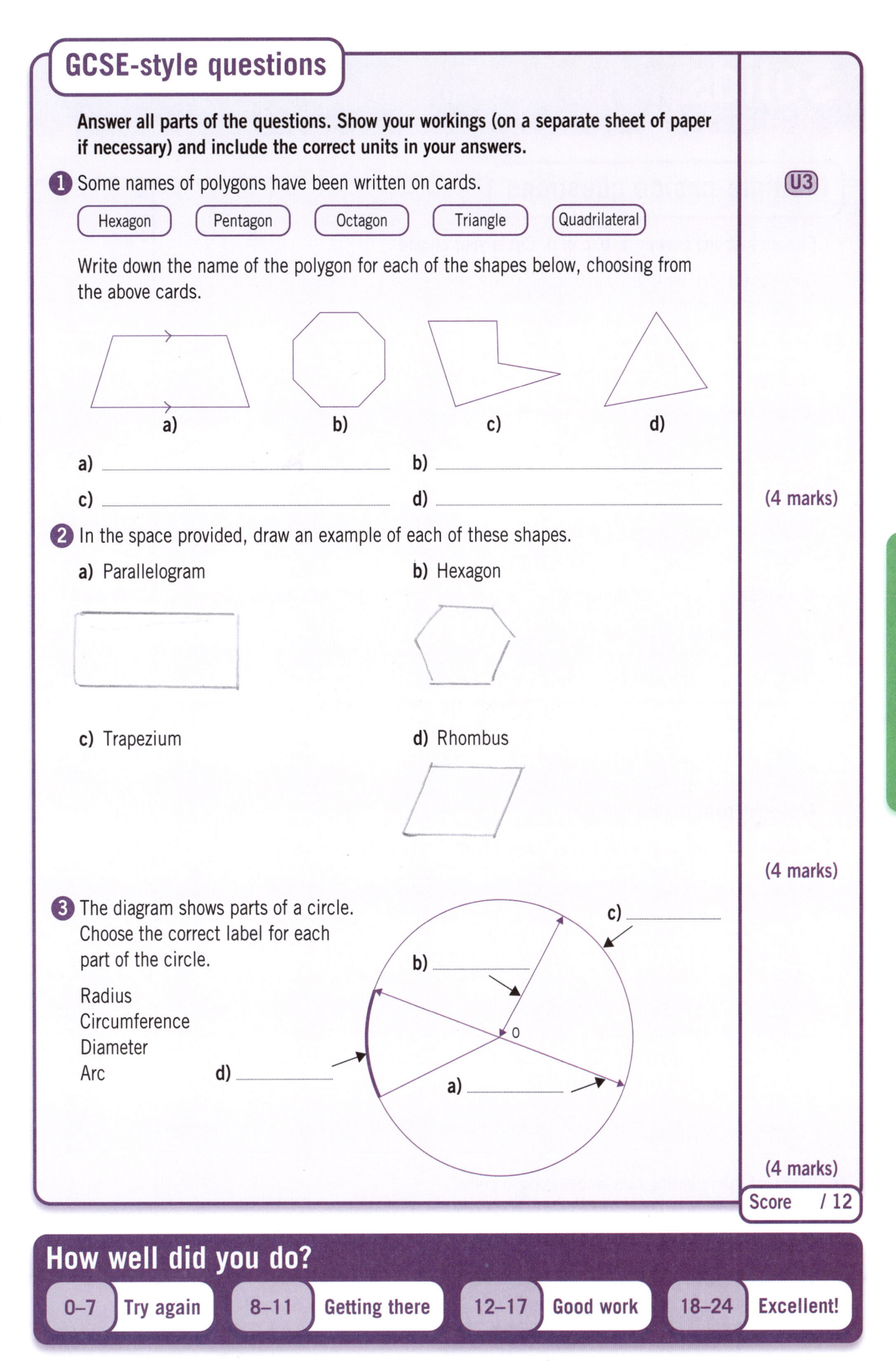

GCSE-style questions

Answer all parts of the questions. Show your workings (on a separate sheet of paper if necessary) and include the correct units in your answers.

1 Some names of polygons have been written on cards.

| Hexagon | Pentagon | Octagon | Triangle | Quadrilateral |

Write down the name of the polygon for each of the shapes below, choosing from the above cards.

a) .... b) ....

c) .... d) ....

(4 marks)

2 In the space provided, draw an example of each of these shapes.

a) Parallelogram

b) Hexagon

c) Trapezium

d) Rhombus

(4 marks)

3 The diagram shows parts of a circle. Choose the correct label for each part of the circle.

Radius
Circumference
Diameter
Arc

a) ....
b) ....
c) ....
d) ....

(4 marks)

Score   / 12

How well did you do?

| 0–7 | Try again | 8–11 | Getting there | 12–17 | Good work | 18–24 | Excellent! |

For more information on this topic, see pages 66–67 of your Success Revision Guide.

Solids

Multiple-choice questions

Choose just one answer, a, b, c or d. Circle your choice.

Questions 1–5 refer to the diagrams opposite.

① What is the name of shape C?

 a) Cube b) Cuboid c) Cone d) Cylinder (1 mark)

② What is the name of shape D?

 a) Cube b) Sphere c) Cuboid d) Cone (1 mark)

③ What is the name of shape A?

 a) Rhombus b) Cone c) Cylinder d) Sphere (1 mark)

④ If you draw a plan of shape A, what shape will it be?

 a) Pentagon b) Heptagon c) Circle d) Rectangle (1 mark)

⑤ How many edges does shape B have?

 a) 12 b) 8 c) 9 d) 10 (1 mark)

Score / 5

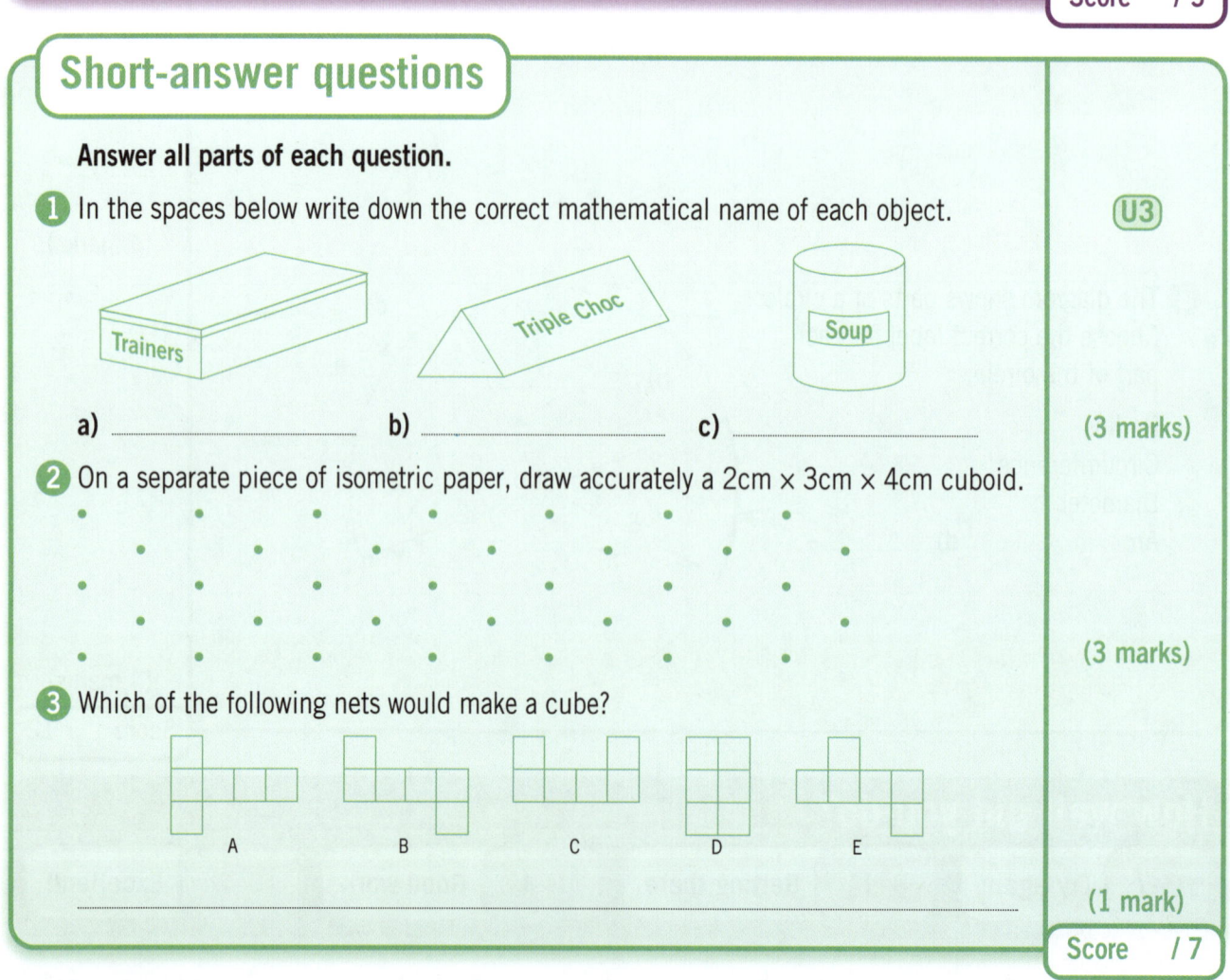

Short-answer questions

Answer all parts of each question.

① In the spaces below write down the correct mathematical name of each object.

 a) _____ b) _____ c) _____ (3 marks)

② On a separate piece of isometric paper, draw accurately a 2cm × 3cm × 4cm cuboid. (3 marks)

③ Which of the following nets would make a cube?

 A   B   C   D   E

 _____ (1 mark)

Score / 7

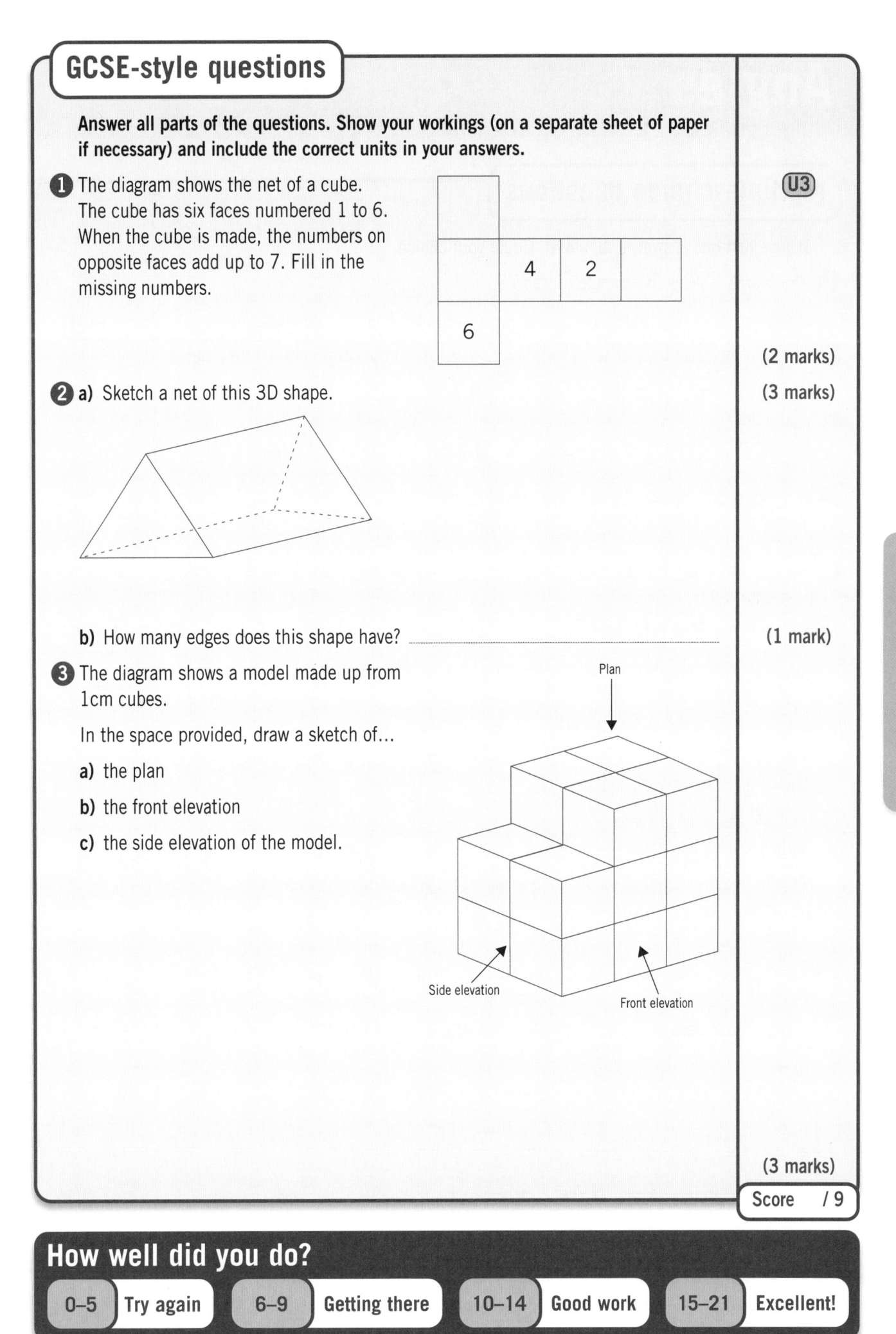

GCSE-style questions

Answer all parts of the questions. Show your workings (on a separate sheet of paper if necessary) and include the correct units in your answers.

1 The diagram shows the net of a cube. The cube has six faces numbered 1 to 6. When the cube is made, the numbers on opposite faces add up to 7. Fill in the missing numbers.

(U3)

(2 marks)

2 a) Sketch a net of this 3D shape. (3 marks)

b) How many edges does this shape have? _____ (1 mark)

3 The diagram shows a model made up from 1cm cubes.

In the space provided, draw a sketch of...

a) the plan

b) the front elevation

c) the side elevation of the model.

(3 marks)

Score / 9

How well did you do?

| 0–5 | Try again | 6–9 | Getting there | 10–14 | Good work | 15–21 | Excellent! |

For more information on this topic, see pages 68–69 of your Success Revision Guide.

Angles

Multiple-choice questions

Choose just one answer, a, b, c or d. Circle your choice.

1. What name is given to an angle of size 72°?
   a) acute   b) obtuse   c) reflex   d) right angle   (1 mark)

2. When shapes tessellate, what is the total of the angles at the point at which they meet?
   a) 180°   b) 90°   c) 360°   d) 270°   (1 mark)

3. Two angles in a scalene triangle are 104° and 39°. What is the size of the third angle?
   a) 217°   b) 37°   c) 57°   d) 157°   (1 mark)

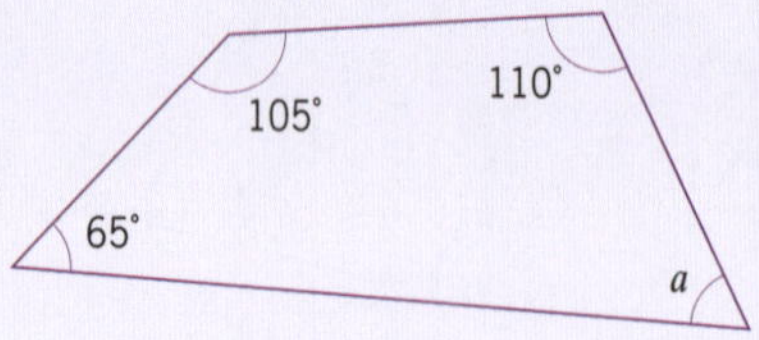

4. In the diagram opposite, what is the size of angle a?
   a) 90°   b) 80°   c) 75°   d) 100°   (1 mark)

5. The size of the exterior angle of a regular polygon is 20°. How many sides does the polygon have?
   a) 18   b) 15   c) 10   d) 20   (1 mark)

Score / 5

Short-answer questions

Answer all parts of each question.

1. Here are the sizes of some angles, written on cards.

   148°   60°   91°   63°   154°   65°   68°

   Match the correct card to the missing angle n in each of the diagrams.

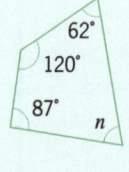

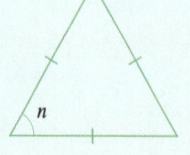

   a) 115°, n — $n = $ _____°
   b) triangle with 54°, n — $n = $ _____°
   c) 105°, 107°, n — $n = $ _____°
   d) crossing lines 112°, n — $n = $ _____°
   e) quadrilateral 62°, 120°, 87°, n — $n = $ _____°
   f) triangle, n — $n = $ _____°
   g) pentagon 100°, 96°, 130°, 87°, 153°, n — $n = $ _____°

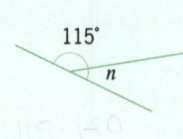

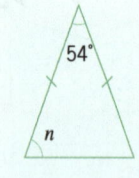

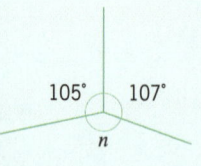

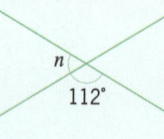

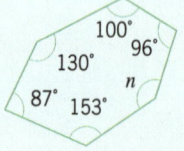

   (7 marks)

2. On the grid, draw six more shapes to continue this tessellation.

   (3 marks)

Score / 10

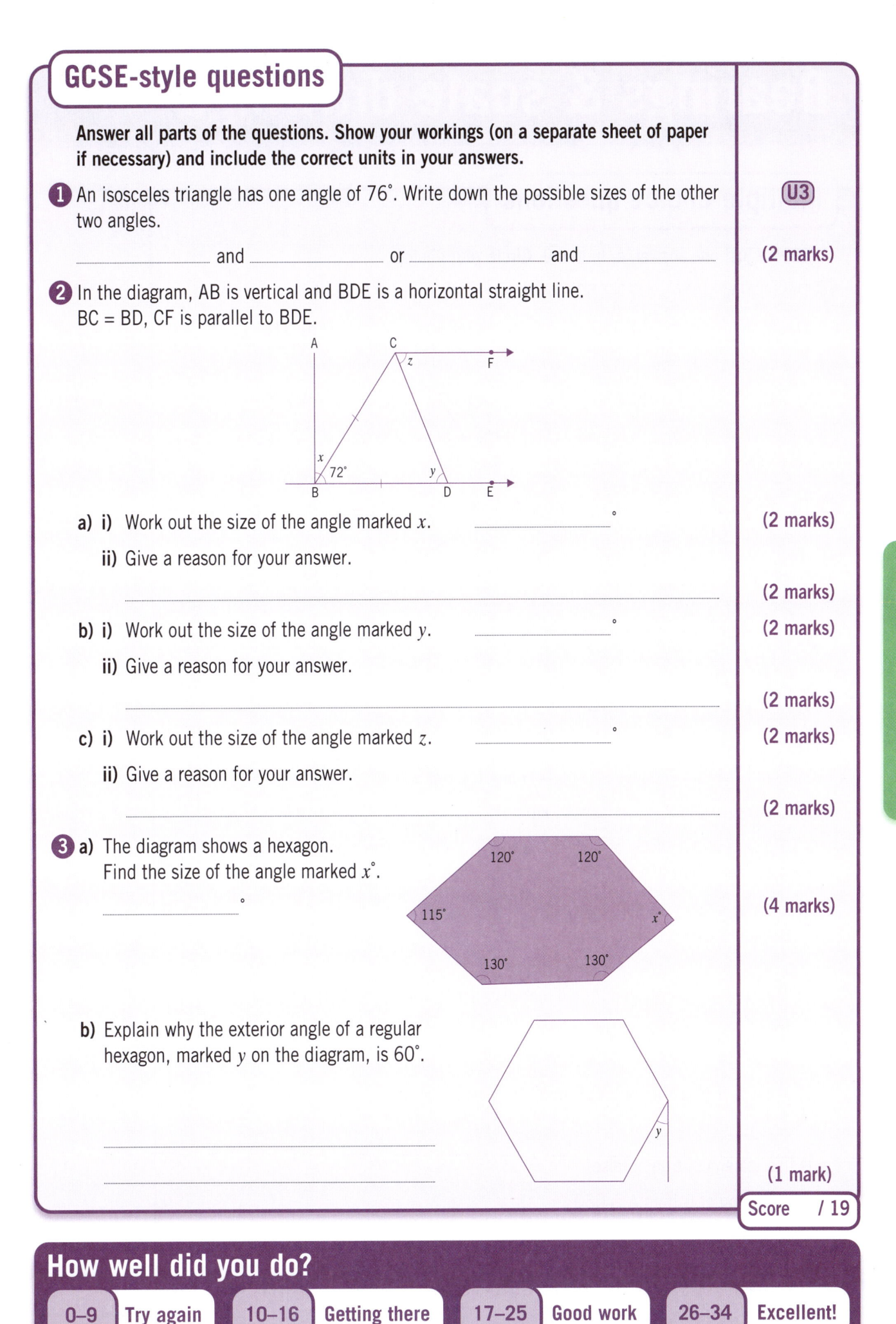

GCSE-style questions

Answer all parts of the questions. Show your workings (on a separate sheet of paper if necessary) and include the correct units in your answers.

1 An isosceles triangle has one angle of 76°. Write down the possible sizes of the other two angles.

_____ and _____ or _____ and _____ (2 marks)

2 In the diagram, AB is vertical and BDE is a horizontal straight line. BC = BD, CF is parallel to BDE.

a) i) Work out the size of the angle marked x. _____ ° (2 marks)

ii) Give a reason for your answer.

_____ (2 marks)

b) i) Work out the size of the angle marked y. _____ ° (2 marks)

ii) Give a reason for your answer.

_____ (2 marks)

c) i) Work out the size of the angle marked z. _____ ° (2 marks)

ii) Give a reason for your answer.

_____ (2 marks)

3 a) The diagram shows a hexagon. Find the size of the angle marked $x°$.

_____ ° (4 marks)

b) Explain why the exterior angle of a regular hexagon, marked y on the diagram, is 60°.

_____
_____ (1 mark)

Score / 19

How well did you do?

0–9 Try again   10–16 Getting there   17–25 Good work   26–34 Excellent!

For more information on this topic, see pages 67 and 70–71 of your Success Revision Guide.

Bearings & scale drawings

Multiple-choice questions

Choose just one answer, a, b, c or d. Circle your choice.

1 The bearing of P from Q is 050°. What is the bearing of Q from P?

a) 130°   b) 050°   c) 230°   d) 310°

(1 mark)

2 The bearing of R from S is 130°. What is the bearing of S from R?

a) 310°   b) 230°   c) 050°   d) 200°

(1 mark)

3 The bearing of A from B is 240°. What is the bearing of B from A?

a) 120°   b) 60°   c) 320°   d) 060°

(1 mark)

4 The length of a car park is 25 metres. A scale diagram of the car park is being drawn to a scale of 1cm to 5 metres. What is the length of the car park on the scale diagram?

a) 500mm   b) 5cm   c) 50cm   d) 5m

(1 mark)

Score / 4

Short-answer questions

Answer all parts of each question.

1 The scale on a road map is 1 : 50 000. Two towns are 20cm apart on the map. Work out the real distance, in km, between the two towns.

_____ km

(2 marks)

2 A ship sails on a bearing of 065° for 10km. It then continues on a bearing of 120° for a further 15km to a port (P).

a) On a separate piece of paper, draw, using a scale of 1cm to 2km, an accurate scale drawing of this information.

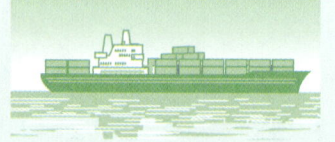

(3 marks)

b) Measure on your diagram the direct distance between the starting point and port P.

_____ km

(1 mark)

c) What is the bearing of port P from the starting point?

_____ °

(1 mark)

3 Is this statement **true** or **false**?

'The bearing of B from A is 060°.'

(1 mark)

Score / 8

GCSE-style questions

Answer all parts of the questions. Show your workings (on a separate sheet of paper if necessary) and include the correct units in your answers.

1 An architect is designing a triangular playground on a piece of land. The diagram shows a scale drawing of one side AB of the playground, ABC.

(U3)

Scale: 1cm represents 30m

a) Use the diagram to calculate the actual distance from A to B. .... (2 marks)

b) Measure and write down the three-figure bearing of B from A. .... (1 mark)

c) The bearing of C from A is 160°. The actual distance from A to C is 135 metres. Plot the point C on the diagram. (2 marks)

2 Here is a sketch of a triangle. Use a compass and a ruler to make an accurate scale drawing of the triangle. Use a scale of 1cm to 2m. The line AB has been drawn for you below.

Diagram not accurately drawn

9m, 12m, 14m (triangle ABC)

A ———————————— B
            14m

(3 marks)

Score / 8

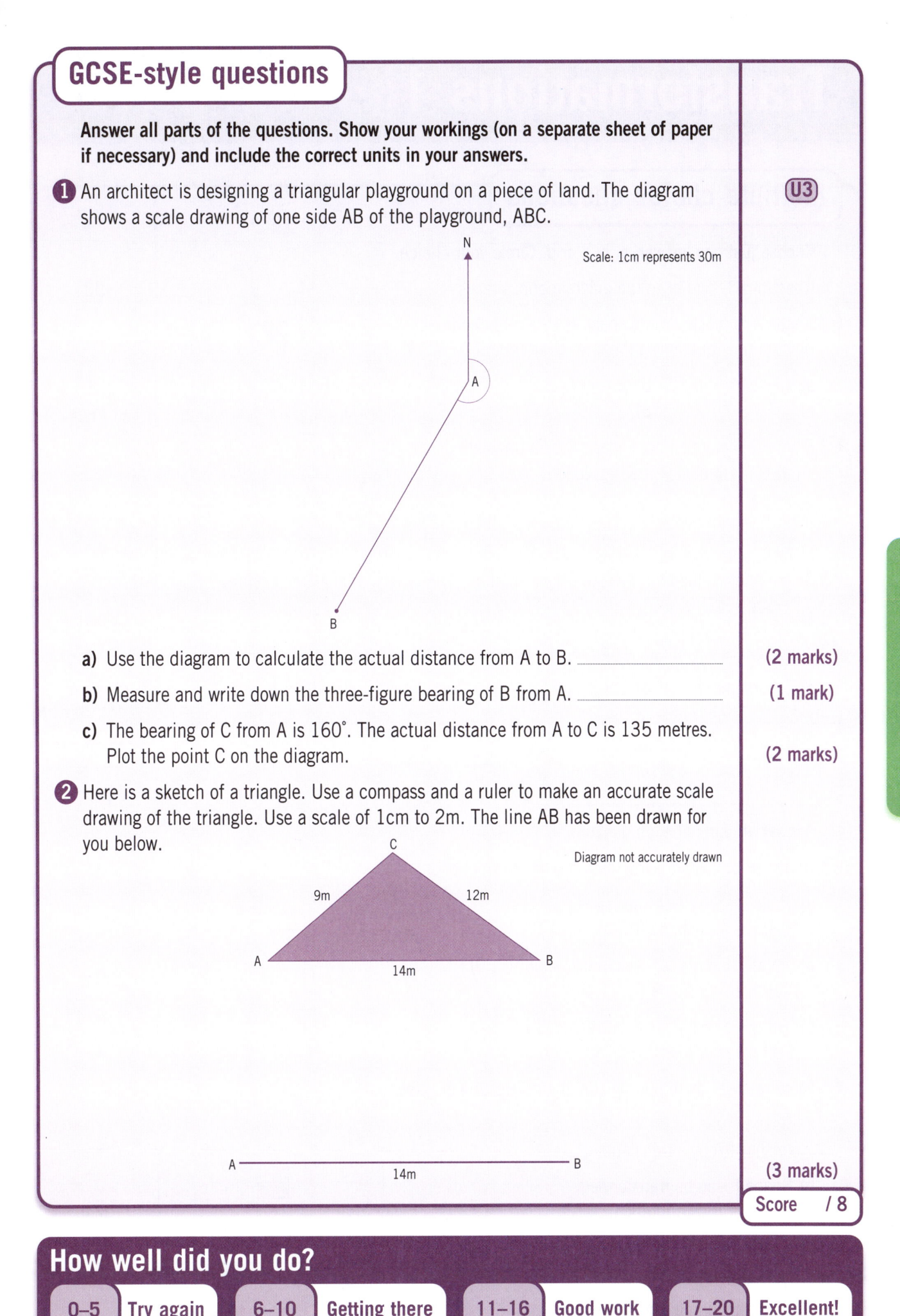

How well did you do?

| 0–5 | Try again | 6–10 | Getting there | 11–16 | Good work | 17–20 | Excellent! |

For more information on this topic, see pages 72–73 of your Success Revision Guide.

Transformations 1

Multiple-choice questions

Choose just one answer, a, b, c or d. Circle your choice.

Questions 1–4 refer to the diagram opposite.

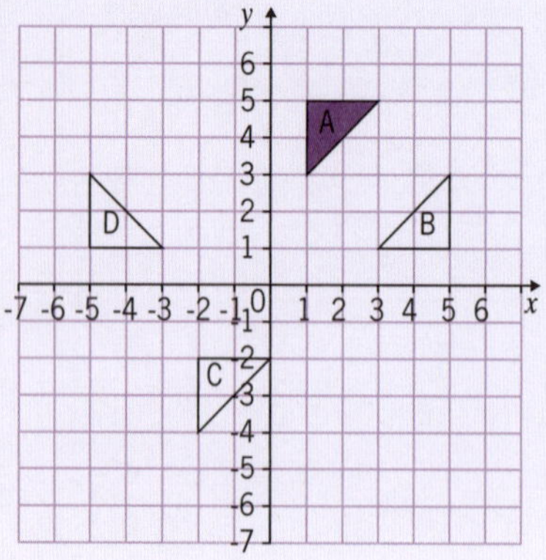

1 Shape A is mapped onto shape B by a reflection. What is the equation of the line of reflection?

a) $y = 1$ b) $x = 2$
c) $y = x$ d) $y = -x$

(1 mark)

2 Shape A is mapped onto shape C by a translation. What is the vector of the translation?

a) $\binom{3}{7}$ b) $\binom{-7}{3}$
c) $\binom{7}{3}$ d) $\binom{-3}{-7}$

(1 mark)

3 Shape A is mapped onto shape D by a rotation. Through what angle is it rotated?

a) 110°   b) 55°   c) 180°   d) 90°

(1 mark)

4 What special name is given to the relationship between triangles A, B, C and D?

a) Enlargement   b) Congruent   c) Translation   d) Similar

(1 mark)

Score / 4

Short-answer questions

Answer all parts of each question.

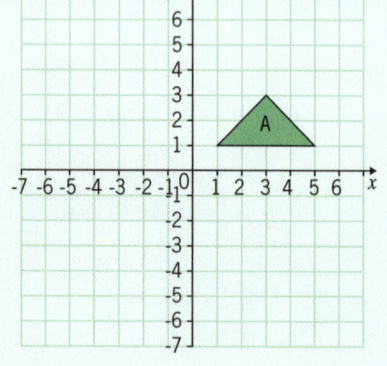

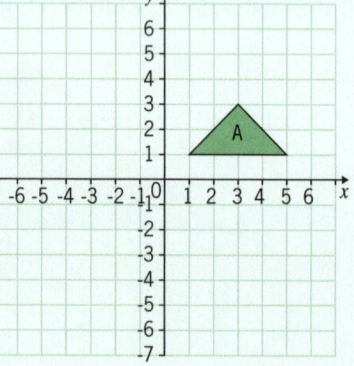

1 On the grid, carry out the following transformations.

a) Reflect shape A in the y-axis.
Call the new shape R. (1 mark)

b) Rotate shape A 90° clockwise, about (0, 0).
Call the new shape S. (1 mark)

c) Translate shape A by the vector $\binom{-3}{4}$.
Call the new shape T. (1 mark)

2 State whether the following statements are **true** or **false**.

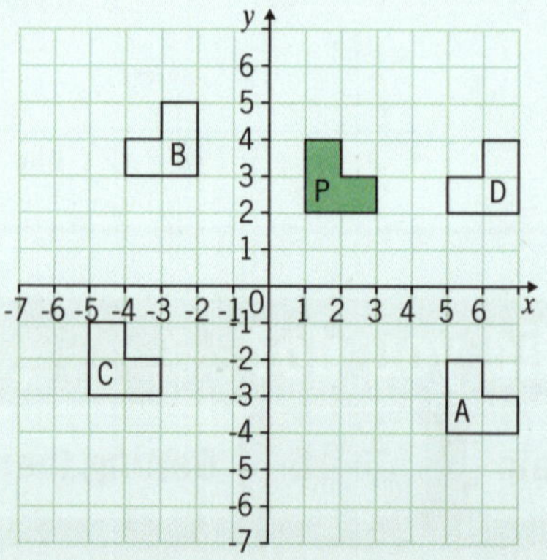

a) Shape P can be transformed to shape A by a translation. _____ (1 mark)

b) Shape P can be transformed to shape B by a rotation. _____ (1 mark)

c) Shape P can be transformed to shape C by a reflection. _____ (1 mark)

d) Shape P can be transformed to shape D by a reflection. _____ (1 mark)

Score / 7

GCSE-style questions

Answer all parts of the questions. Show your workings (on a separate sheet of paper if necessary) and include the correct units in your answers.

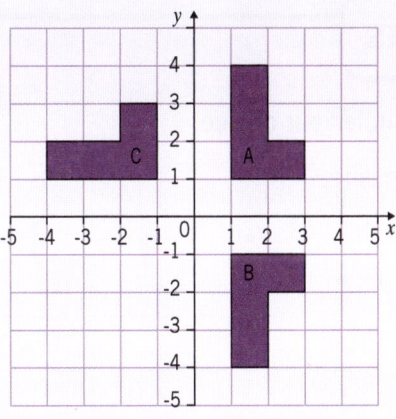

1

U3

a) Describe fully the single transformation that takes shape A onto shape B.

(2 marks)

b) Describe fully the single transformation that takes shape A onto shape C.

(3 marks)

2

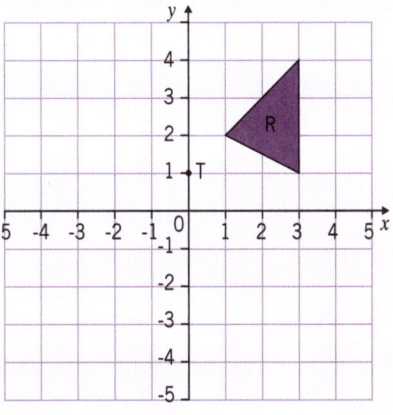

The triangle R has been drawn on the grid.

a) Rotate triangle R 90° clockwise about the point T (0, 1) and call the image P. (3 marks)

b) Translate triangle R by the vector $\begin{pmatrix} -4 \\ -3 \end{pmatrix}$ and call the image Q. (3 marks)

Score / 11

How well did you do?

0–6 Try again | 7–10 Getting there | 11–16 Good work | 17–22 Excellent!

For more information on this topic, see pages 74–77 of your Success Revision Guide.

Transformations 2

Multiple-choice questions

Choose just one answer, a, b, c or d. Circle your choice.

Questions 1–3 refer to the diagram opposite.

1 Shape Q is enlarged to give shape P. What is the scale factor of the enlargement?

a) $\frac{1}{3}$ b) 2   c) 3   d) $\frac{1}{2}$ (1 mark)

2 What are the coordinates of the centre of enlargement?

a) (3, -2)   b) (-2, 3)   c) (-3, 4)   d) (0, 0)   (1 mark)

3 What is the single transformation that would map shape Q onto shape R?

a) Reflection   b) Rotation   c) Translation   d) Enlargement   (1 mark)

Score / 3

Short-answer questions

Answer all parts of each question.

1 Draw an enlargement of shape R, with centre O and scale factor 3. Call the image P.

(3 marks)

2 The diagram shows the position of three shapes, A, B and C.

a) Describe the transformation that moves A onto C.

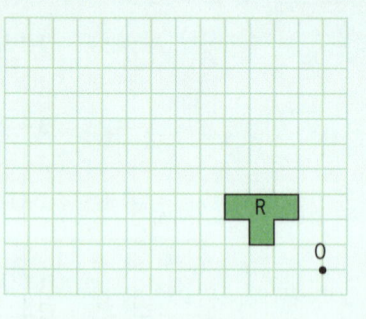

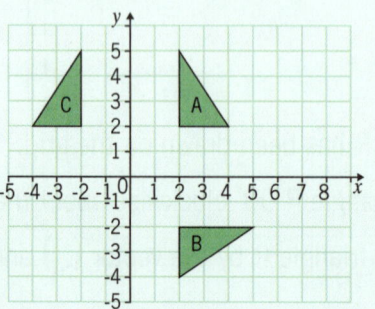

_____

_____

(2 marks)

b) Describe the transformation that moves A onto B.

_____

_____

(2 marks)

c) Describe the transformation that moves B onto C.

_____

_____

(2 marks)

Score / 9

GCSE-style questions

Answer all parts of the questions. Show your workings (on a separate sheet of paper if necessary) and include the correct units in your answers.

1 a) Draw an enlargement of the shape. Use a scale factor of 2. Call the enlarged shape A.

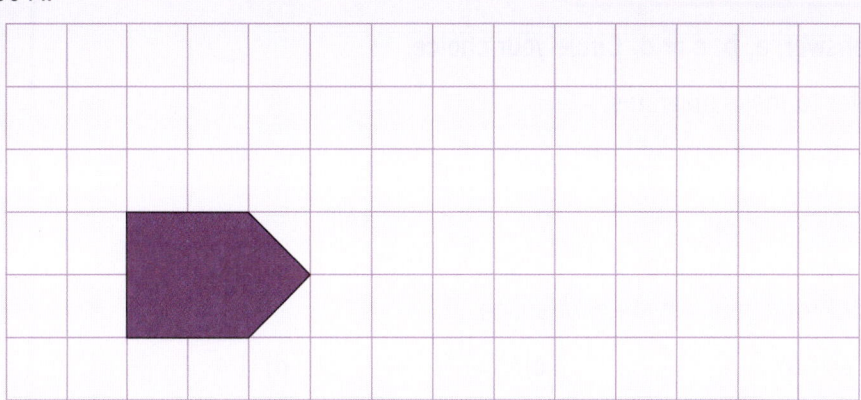

(U3)

(2 marks)

b) If the area of the original shape is 5cm², what is the area of the enlarged shape?

_____ cm² (1 mark)

2 a) Enlarge triangle N by a scale factor of 3 with centre R (-6, 7). Call the image P. (3 marks)

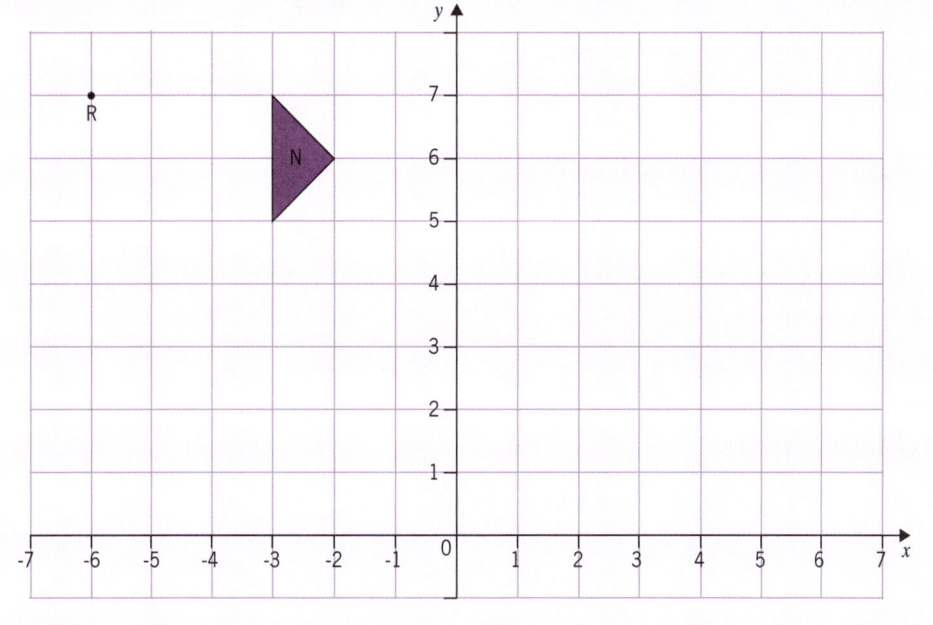

b) Daniel says that shapes N and P are congruent. Explain whether Daniel is right.

_____

_____

(1 mark)

Score / 7

How well did you do?

| 0–3 | Try again | 4–8 | Getting there | 9–13 | Good work | 14–19 | Excellent! |

For more information on this topic, see pages 74–77 of your Success Revision Guide.

Symmetry & constructions

Multiple-choice questions

Choose just one answer, a, b, c or d. Circle your choice.

Questions 1–5 refer to these diagrams.

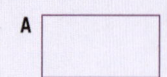

A   B   C

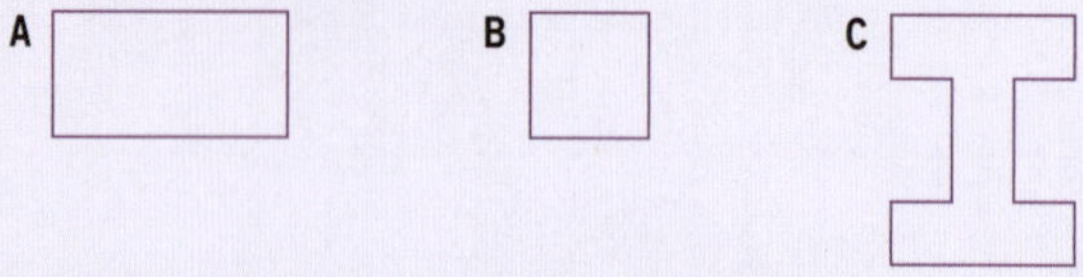

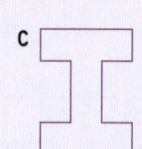

1 What is the order of rotational symmetry of shape B?

a) 4   b) 2   c) 3   d) 1   (1 mark)

2 How many lines of symmetry does shape A have?

a) 5   b) 4   c) 3   d) 2   (1 mark)

3 How many lines of symmetry does shape B have?

a) 4   b) 3   c) 2   d) 1   (1 mark)

4 What is the order of rotational symmetry of shape C?

a) 1   b) 3   c) 2   d) 4   (1 mark)

5 How many lines of symmetry does shape C have?

a) 4   b) 2   c) 3   d) 1   (1 mark)

U3

Score / 5

Short-answer questions

Answer all parts of each question.

1 Draw in one line of symmetry on each of the shapes below.

a)   b)

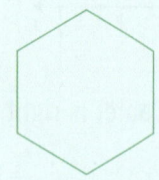

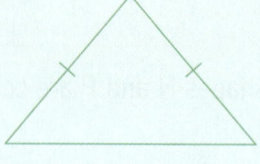

(2 marks)

2 a) Using a pair of compasses only, bisect this angle.

(2 marks)

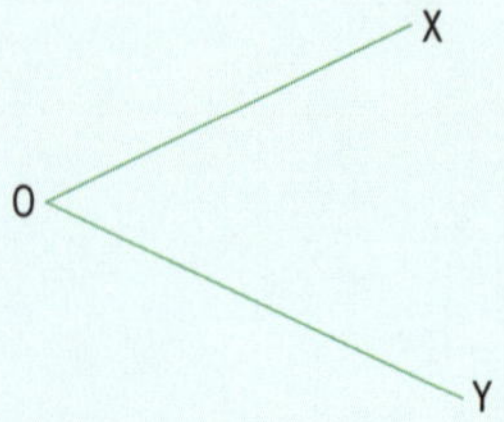

b) Measure angle XOY.

_____

(1 mark)

3 On a separate piece of paper, using a ruler and a pair of compasses only, make an accurate drawing of this triangle.

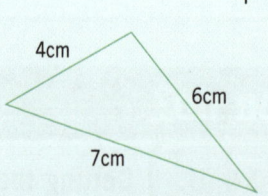

4cm   6cm   7cm

(3 marks)

U3

Score / 8

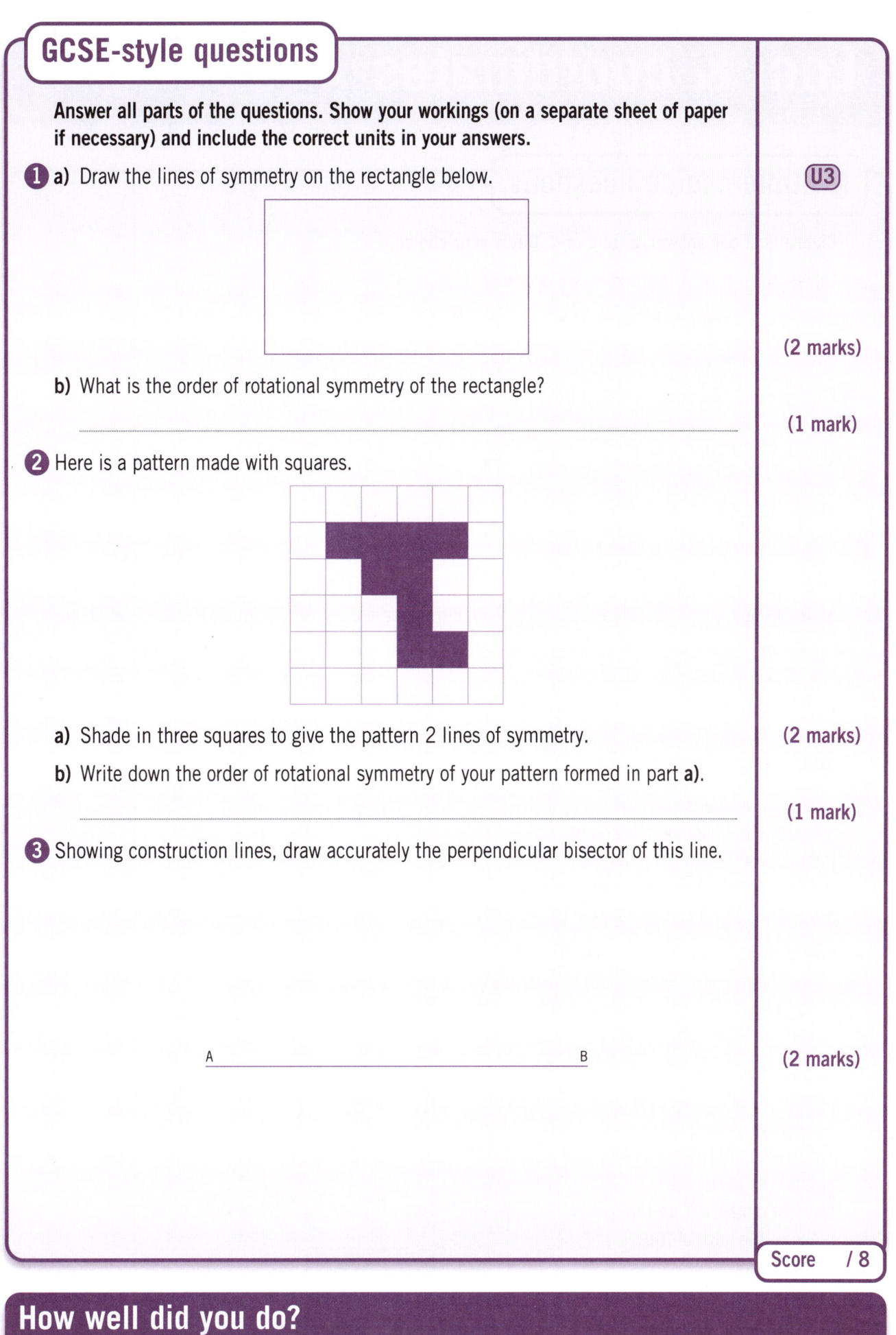

GCSE-style questions

Answer all parts of the questions. Show your workings (on a separate sheet of paper if necessary) and include the correct units in your answers.

1 a) Draw the lines of symmetry on the rectangle below.

(2 marks)

b) What is the order of rotational symmetry of the rectangle?

....

(1 mark)

2 Here is a pattern made with squares.

a) Shade in three squares to give the pattern 2 lines of symmetry. (2 marks)

b) Write down the order of rotational symmetry of your pattern formed in part **a)**.

....

(1 mark)

3 Showing construction lines, draw accurately the perpendicular bisector of this line.

A ——————————————————————— B

(2 marks)

Score   / 8

How well did you do?

| 0–6 | Try again | 7–11 | Getting there | 12–16 | Good work | 17–21 | Excellent! |

For more information on this topic, see pages 78–79 of your Success Revision Guide.

Loci & coordinates

Multiple-choice questions

Choose just one answer, a, b, c or d. Circle your choice.

Questions 1–4 refer to the diagram opposite.

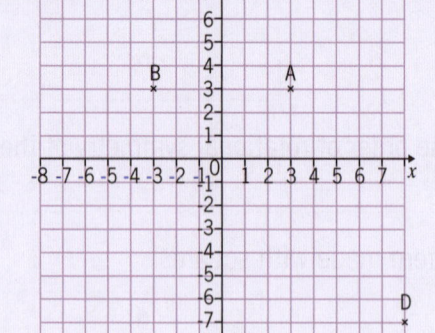

1 What are the coordinates of point A?

   a) (-3, 3)   b) (-7, 8)   c) (3, 3)   d) (8, -7)   (1 mark)

2 What are the coordinates of point B?

   a) (-3, 3)   b) (-7, 8)   c) (3, 3)   d) (8, -7)   (1 mark)

3 What are the coordinates of point D?

   a) (-3, 3)   b) (-7, 8)   c) (3, 3)   d) (8, -7)   (1 mark)

4 Point C, which is the vertex of a quadrilateral ABCD, is at (-6, -7). What is the name of the quadrilateral ABCD?

   a) Rectangle   b) Trapezium   c) Parallelogram   d) Rhombus   (1 mark)

Score / 4

Short-answer questions

Answer all parts of each question.

1 The diagram shows the position of the post office (P), the hospital (H) and the school (S). Robert lives less than 4 miles from the hospital, less than 5 miles from the post office and less than 8 miles from the school.

Use shading to show the area where Robert lives. Use a scale of 1 grid square = 1 mile.

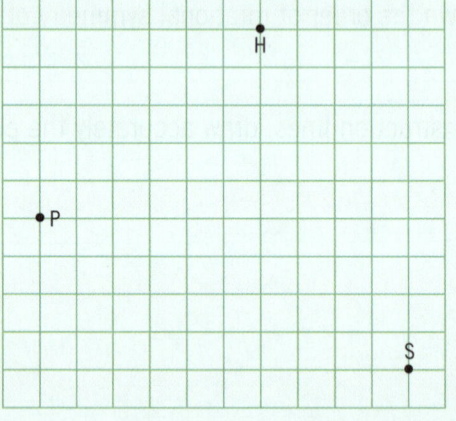

(4 marks)

2 In the scale drawing opposite, the shaded area represents a fish pond. There is a wire fence all around the pond. The shortest distance from the fence to the edge of the pond is always 2m.

On the diagram, draw accurately the position of the fence. Use a scale of 1 grid square = 1m.

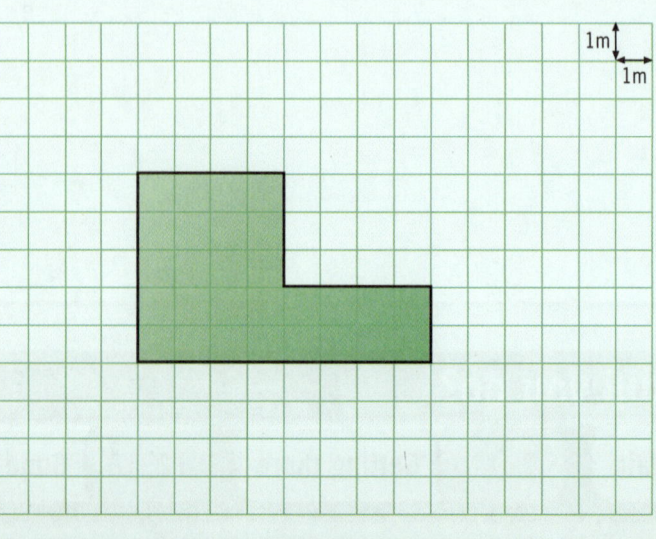

(3 marks)

Score / 7

GCSE-style questions

Answer all parts of the questions. Show your workings (on a separate sheet of paper if necessary) and include the correct units in your answers.

1 In this question you should use a ruler and a pair of compasses only for the constructions.

Triangle ABC is the plan of an adventure playground.

P is an ice-cream kiosk inside the adventure playground.
P is the same distance from A as it is from C.
P is the same distance from AC as it is from AB.
On the diagram clearly mark the point P with a cross.

(U3)

(3 marks)

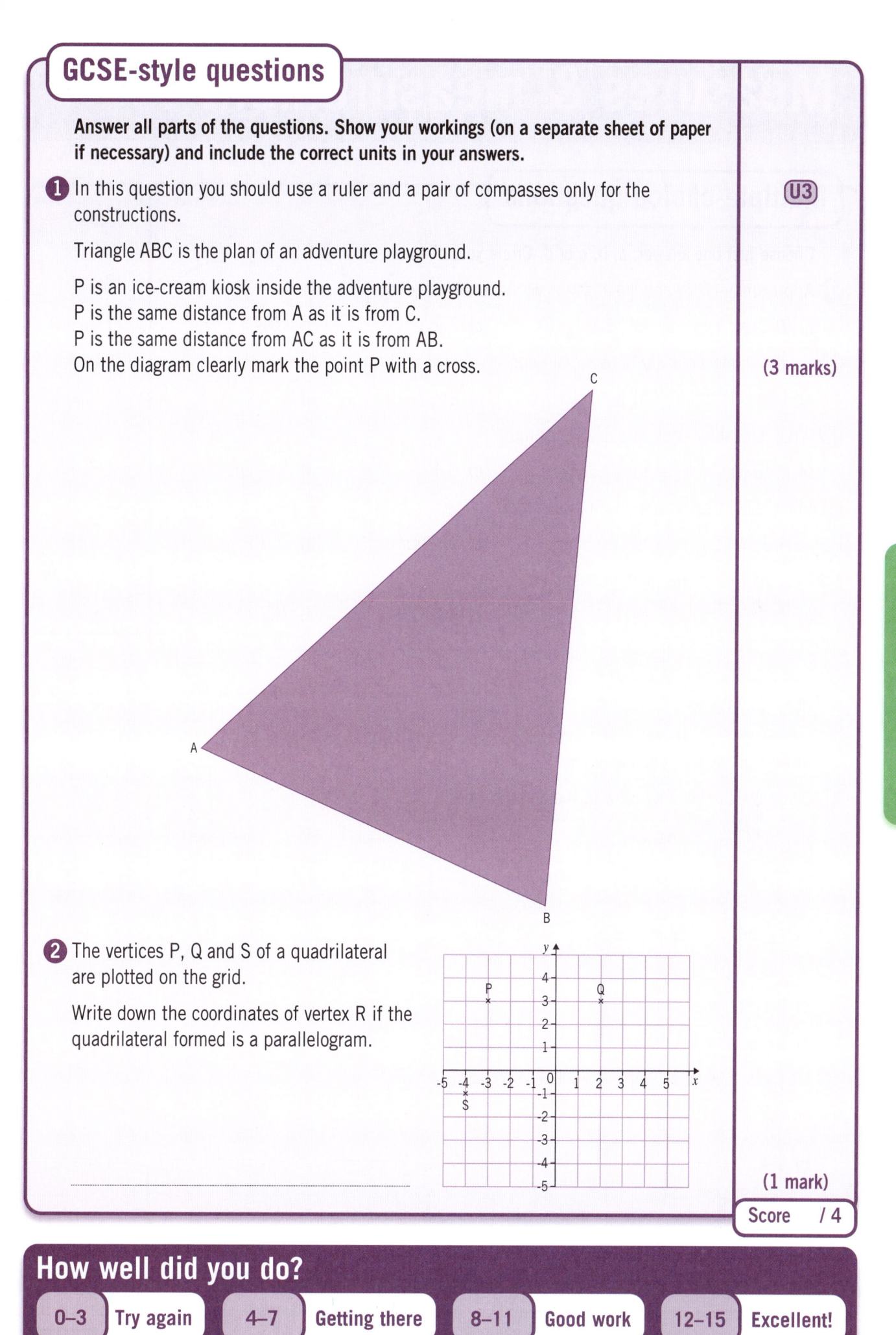

2 The vertices P, Q and S of a quadrilateral are plotted on the grid.

Write down the coordinates of vertex R if the quadrilateral formed is a parallelogram.

(1 mark)

Score / 4

How well did you do?

| 0–3 Try again | 4–7 Getting there | 8–11 Good work | 12–15 Excellent! |

For more information on this topic, see pages 80–81 of your Success Revision Guide.

Measures & measurement 1

Multiple-choice questions

Choose just one answer, a, b, c or d. Circle your choice.

1 Approximately how many kilograms would an 'average' man weigh?

a) 720kg   b) 72kg   c) 7.2kg   d) 45kg   (1 mark)

2 How many seconds are in three minutes?

a) 180   b) 60   c) 240   d) 120   (1 mark)

3 What is 1842 written as a 12-hour time?

a) 6.42am   b) 6.15am   c) 6.42   d) 6.42pm   (1 mark)

4 What is 5.25am written in 24-hour time?

a) 5.25pm   b) 0525am   c) 0525pm   d) 0525   (1 mark)

5 How many days are there in a leap year?

a) 366   b) 364   c) 365   d) 367   (1 mark)

Score   / 5

Short-answer questions

Answer all parts of each question.

1 Complete the table below with the correct times.

12-hour clock	4.23pm			3.16pm		9.38pm
24-hour clock		1534	2126		0314	

(2 marks)

2 Using metric units, estimate...

a) the length of your classroom   (1 mark)

b) the distance from Manchester to London   (1 mark)

c) the volume of medicine on a medicine spoon.   (1 mark)

3 On the scales below, mark the following readings.

a) 6.7   (scale 6 to 7)   (1 mark)

b) 9.4   (scale 9 to 11)   (1 mark)

c) 12.75   (scale 12 to 14)   (1 mark)

d) 7.34   (scale 7.2 to 7.4)   (1 mark)

Score   / 9

GCSE-style questions

Answer all parts of the questions. Show your workings (on a separate sheet of paper if necessary) and include the correct units in your answers.

1 a) Write down the reading marked with an arrow on this meter.

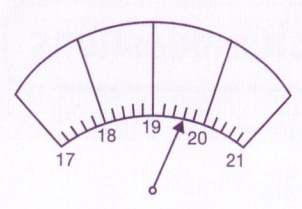

.... (1 mark)

b) Write down the reading marked with an arrow on this scale.

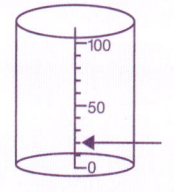

.... (1 mark)

c) Find the number 16 on the number line. Mark it with an arrow (↓).

(1 mark)

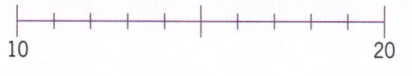

d) Find the number 12.4 on the number line. Mark it with an arrow (↓).

(1 mark)

2 Part of a train timetable is shown.

Manchester	1415		1521	
Stafford	1503		1612	
Milton Keynes	1555	1605	1701	1715
Watford		1638		1748
Euston	1646	1701	1752	1806

Sarah travels from Stafford to Watford. She has to change trains at Milton Keynes.

a) i) Sarah arrives in Stafford at 1541 to catch the next train. How long does she have to wait in Stafford for the next train?

.... minutes (1 mark)

ii) How long does Sarah have to wait at Milton Keynes for the next train to Watford?

.... minutes (2 marks)

b) Briony is travelling from Milton Keynes to Euston. She arrives at Milton Keynes at 1710. What time will she arrive in Euston?

.... (1 mark)

Score / 8

How well did you do?

| 0–6 | Try again | 7–11 | Getting there | 12–16 | Good work | 17–22 | Excellent! |

For more information on this topic, see pages 82–83 of your Success Revision Guide.

Measures & measurement 2

Multiple-choice questions

Choose just one answer, a, b, c or d. Circle your choice.

1) What is 2500g in kilograms?
   a) 25kg   b) 2.5kg   c) 0.25kg   d) 250kg   (1 mark)

2) Daisy is 165cm tall to the nearest cm. What is the lower limit of her height?
   a) 164.5cm   b) 165.5cm   c) 165cm   d) 164.9cm   (1 mark)

3) Approximately how many pounds are in 4kg?
   a) 6.9   b) 12.4   c) 7.7   d) 8.8   (1 mark)

4) A car travels for $2\frac{1}{2}$ hours at a speed of 42mph. How far does the car travel?
   a) 96 miles   b) 100 miles   c) 105 miles   d) 140 miles   (1 mark)

5) What is the speed of a car if it travels 120km in 1 hour 30 minutes?
   a) $1.\dot{3}$km/h   b) 0.75km/h   c) 75km/h   d) 80km/h   (1 mark)

Score / 5

Short-answer questions

Answer all parts of each question.

1) Complete the statements below.
   a) 8km = _____ m
   b) 3250g = _____ kg
   c) 7 tonnes = _____ kg
   d) 52cm = _____ m
   e) 2.7 litres = _____ ml
   f) 262cm = _____ km
   (6 marks)

2) Two towns are approximately 20km apart. Approximately how many miles is this?
   _____ miles (1 mark)

3) A recipe uses 600g of flour. Approximately how many pounds is this?
   _____ lbs (1 mark)

4) Giovanni drove 200 miles in 3 hours and 20 minutes. At what average speed did he travel?
   _____ mph (2 marks)

5) Tamara travels at an average speed of 38mph. Her journey takes 1 hour and 15 minutes. How far does Tamara travel?
   _____ miles (2 marks)

Score / 12

GCSE-style questions

Answer all parts of the questions. Show your workings (on a separate sheet of paper if necessary) and include the correct units in your answers.

1 a) Change 8 kilograms into pounds.

_____ pounds (2 marks)

b) Change 30 miles into kilometres.

_____ km (2 marks)

2 Amy took part in a sponsored walk. She walked from the school to the park and back. The distance from the school to the park is 9km.

a) Amy walked from the school to the park at an average speed of 6km/h. Find the time she took to walk from the school to the park.

_____ minutes (2 marks)

b) Her average speed for the return journey was 4.5km/h. Calculate her average speed for the whole journey. Give your answer to 1 decimal place.

_____ km/h (4 marks)

3 A book has a mass of 112 grams, correct to the nearest gram. Write down the least possible mass of the book.

_____ grams (1 mark)

4 The temperature in a refrigerator is measured as 5°C, to the nearest degree. Write down the lower bound for the temperature.

_____ °C (1 mark)

5 The driving distance between two cities is 70 miles. Rosie travels between the two cities at an average speed of 56mph. How long does the journey take?

(2 marks)

6 The speed limit through some roadworks is 50mph. Cameras recorded the time taken for a car to travel 2400m through the roadworks as 108 seconds. 10mph is approximately 4.47m/s. Was the car speeding through the roadworks? You must show your working.

(5 marks)

Score / 19

How well did you do?

| 0–11 | Try again | 12–19 | Getting there | 20–27 | Good work | 28–36 | Excellent! |

For more information on this topic, see pages 84–85 of your Success Revision Guide.

Pythagoras' theorem

Multiple-choice questions

Choose just one answer, a, b, c or d. Circle your choice.

1 Calculate the missing length y of this triangle.

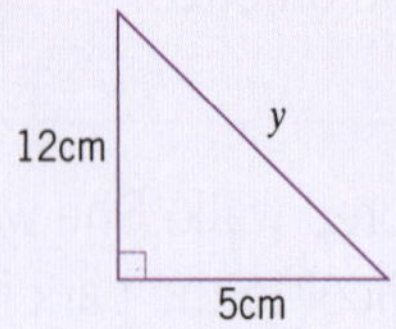

a) 169cm b) 13cm
c) 17cm d) 84.5cm

(1 mark)

2 Calculate the missing length y of this triangle.

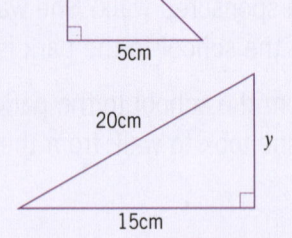

a) 13.2cm b) 5cm
c) 25cm d) 625cm

(1 mark)

3 Point A has coordinates (1, 4) and point B has coordinates (4, 10). What are the coordinates of the midpoint of the line AB?

a) (5, 14) b) (3, 6) c) (2.5, 7) d) (1.5, 3)

(1 mark)

4 Point C had coordinates (3, 6) and point D has coordinates (7, 10). What are the coordinates of the midpoint of the line CD?

a) (5, 2) b) (5, 10) c) (5, 8) d) (10, 16)

(1 mark)

Score / 4

Short-answer questions

Answer all parts of each question.

1 Calculate the missing lengths of these right-angled triangles. Give your answer to 1 decimal place, where appropriate.

a) 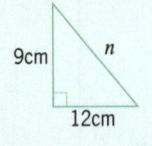 9cm, n, 12cm
b) 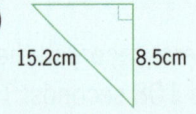 15.2cm, n, 8.5cm
c) 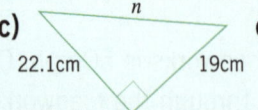 22.1cm, n, 19cm
d) 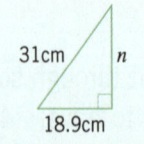 31cm, n, 18.9cm

n = _____ cm   n = _____ cm   n = _____ cm   n = _____ cm

(8 marks)

2 Molly says, 'The angle x° in this triangle is 90°.' Explain how Molly knows this without measuring the size of the angle.

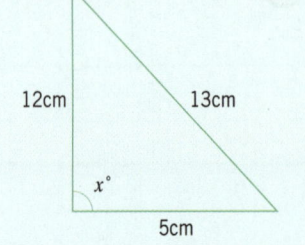

(12cm, 13cm, 5cm, x°)

_____

_____

(2 marks)

3 Colin says, 'The length of this line is 6.7 units (1 d.p.) and the coordinates of the midpoint are (3.5, 8).' Decide whether these statements are **true** or **false**. Give an explanation for your answer.

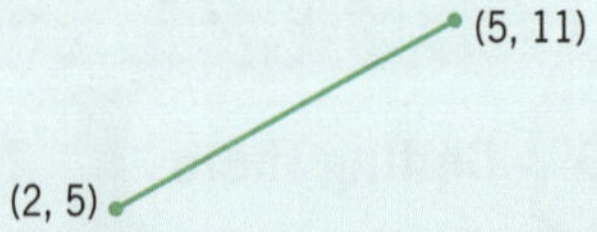

(5, 11)
(2, 5)

_____

_____

(2 marks)

Score / 12

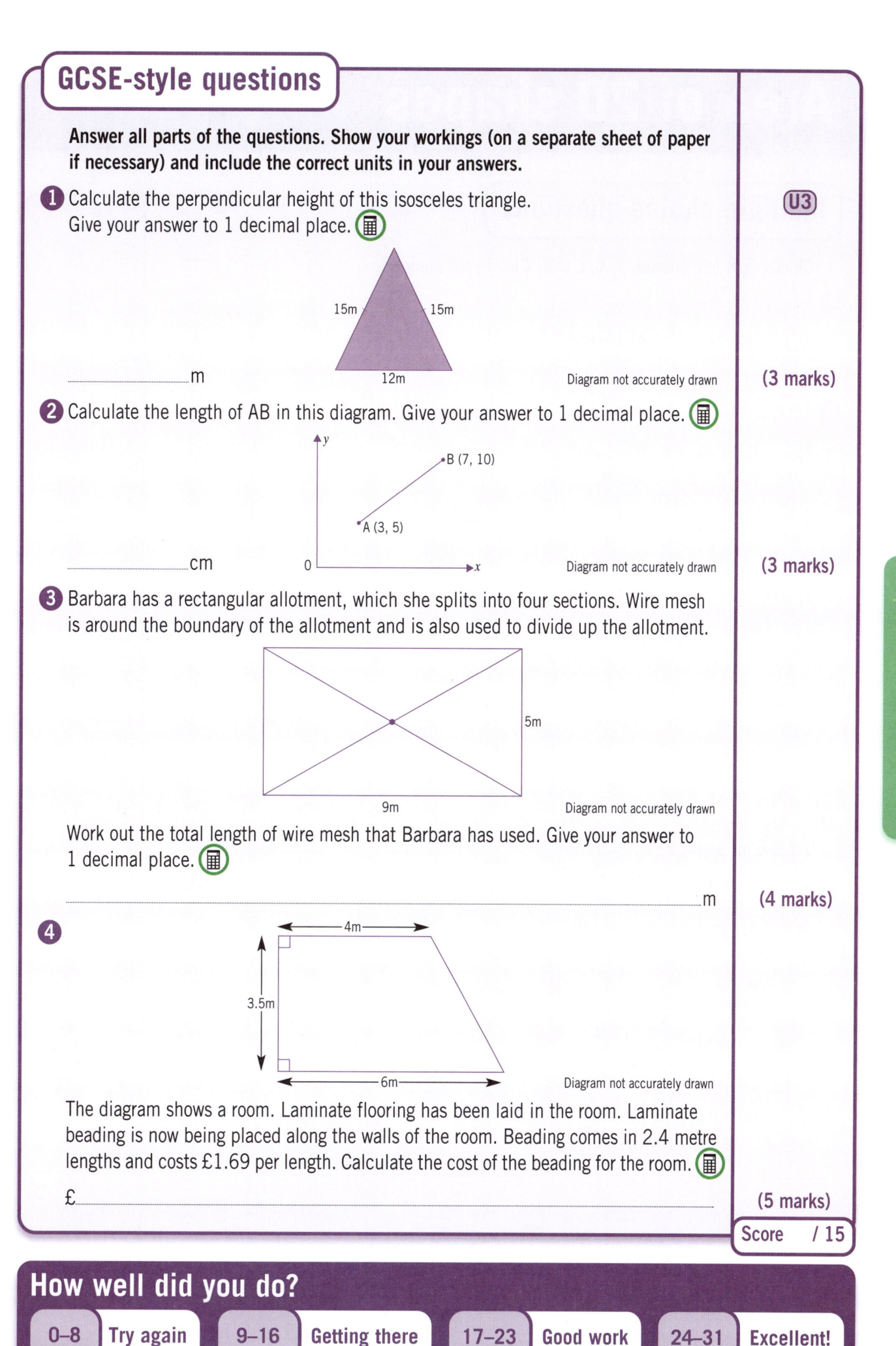

GCSE-style questions

Answer all parts of the questions. Show your workings (on a separate sheet of paper if necessary) and include the correct units in your answers.

1 Calculate the perpendicular height of this isosceles triangle. Give your answer to 1 decimal place.

15m, 15m, 12m
Diagram not accurately drawn

.... m (3 marks)

2 Calculate the length of AB in this diagram. Give your answer to 1 decimal place.

B (7, 10)
A (3, 5)
Diagram not accurately drawn

.... cm (3 marks)

3 Barbara has a rectangular allotment, which she splits into four sections. Wire mesh is around the boundary of the allotment and is also used to divide up the allotment.

5m, 9m
Diagram not accurately drawn

Work out the total length of wire mesh that Barbara has used. Give your answer to 1 decimal place.

.... m (4 marks)

4

4m, 3.5m, 6m
Diagram not accurately drawn

The diagram shows a room. Laminate flooring has been laid in the room. Laminate beading is now being placed along the walls of the room. Beading comes in 2.4 metre lengths and costs £1.69 per length. Calculate the cost of the beading for the room.

£............................ (5 marks)

Score / 15

How well did you do?

| 0–8 Try again | 9–16 Getting there | 17–23 Good work | 24–31 Excellent! |

For more information on this topic, see pages 86–87 of your Success Revision Guide.

Area of 2D shapes

Multiple-choice questions

Choose just one answer, a, b, c or d. Circle your choice.

1. What is the area of this triangle? 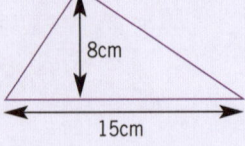
   a) 60mm^2
   b) 120cm^2
   c) 60cm^2
   d) 46cm^2

   (1 mark)

2. What is the approximate circumference of a circle of radius 4cm?
   a) 25.1cm^2
   b) 50.3cm
   c) 12.6cm
   d) 25.1cm

   (1 mark)

3. Change 50 000cm^2 into m^2.
   a) 500m^2
   b) 5m^2
   c) 0.5m^2
   d) 50m^2

   (1 mark)

4. What is the area of this circle? (Use π = 3.14) 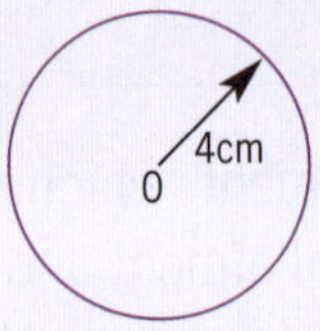
   a) 25.1cm^2
   b) 55cm^2
   c) 12.6cm^2
   d) 50.24cm^2

   (1 mark)

5. If the area of a rectangle is 20cm^2 and its width is 2.5cm, what is its length?
   a) 9cm
   b) 8cm
   c) 7.5cm
   d) 2.5cm

   (1 mark)

Score / 5

Short-answer questions

Answer all parts of each question.

1. For each of the diagrams below, state whether the area given is **true** or **false**.

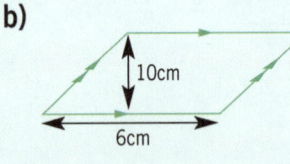

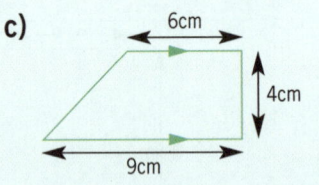

   a) Area = 48cm^2 (triangle, 6cm by 8cm)

   b) Area = 60cm^2 (parallelogram, 10cm by 6cm)

   c) Area = 108cm^2 (parallelogram, 6cm/9cm by 4cm)

   (3 marks)

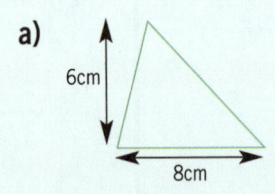

2. Calculate the perimeter of this shape, correct to 1 decimal place. 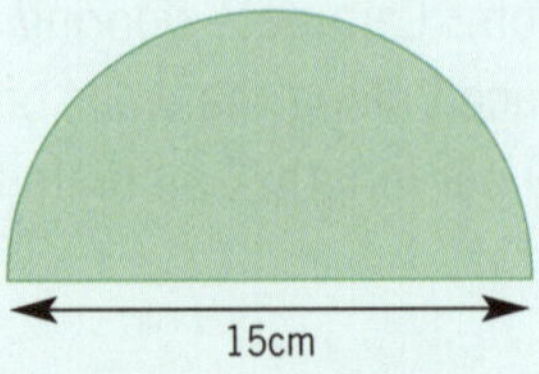

   (semicircle, 15cm)

   _____ cm

   (3 marks)

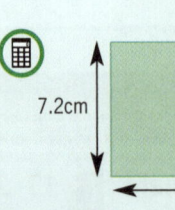

3. Calculate the area of the shaded region. 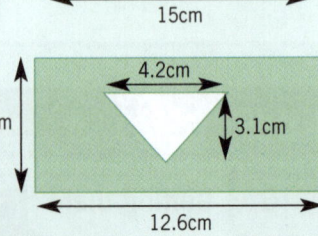

   (rectangle 12.6cm by 7.2cm with triangle 4.2cm by 3.1cm removed)

   _____ cm^2

   (3 marks)

Score / 9

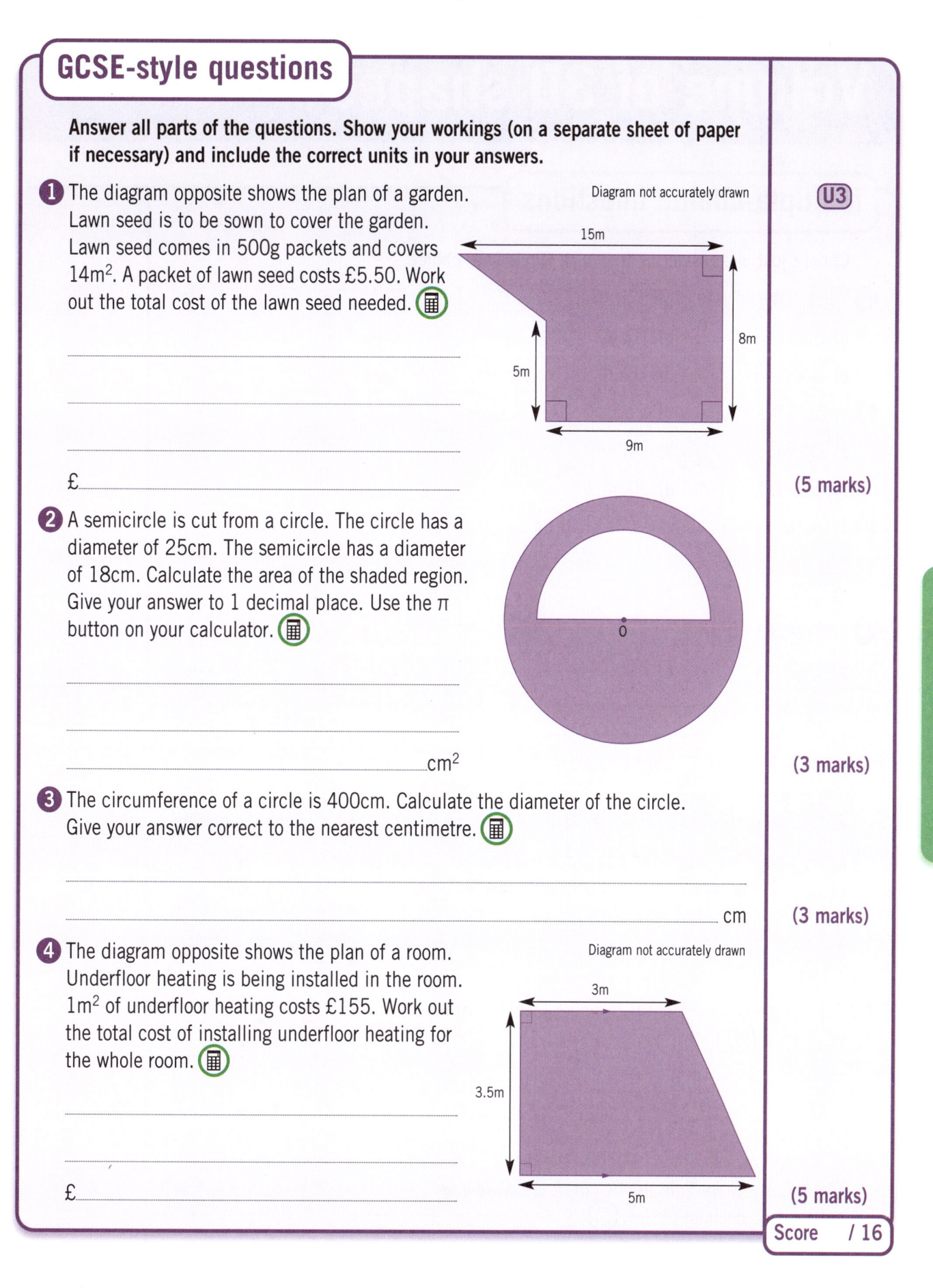

GCSE-style questions

Answer all parts of the questions. Show your workings (on a separate sheet of paper if necessary) and include the correct units in your answers.

1. The diagram opposite shows the plan of a garden. Lawn seed is to be sown to cover the garden. Lawn seed comes in 500g packets and covers 14m². A packet of lawn seed costs £5.50. Work out the total cost of the lawn seed needed.

   Diagram not accurately drawn

   £ .... (5 marks)

2. A semicircle is cut from a circle. The circle has a diameter of 25cm. The semicircle has a diameter of 18cm. Calculate the area of the shaded region. Give your answer to 1 decimal place. Use the π button on your calculator.

   .... cm² (3 marks)

3. The circumference of a circle is 400cm. Calculate the diameter of the circle. Give your answer correct to the nearest centimetre.

   .... cm (3 marks)

4. The diagram opposite shows the plan of a room. Underfloor heating is being installed in the room. 1m² of underfloor heating costs £155. Work out the total cost of installing underfloor heating for the whole room.

   Diagram not accurately drawn

   £ .... (5 marks)

   Score / 16

How well did you do?

| 0–8 Try again | 9–14 Getting there | 15–22 Good work | 23–30 Excellent! |

For more information on this topic, see pages 88–89 of your Success Revision Guide.

Volume of 3D shapes

Multiple-choice questions

Choose just one answer, a, b, c or d. Circle your choice.

1 What is the volume of this cuboid?
   a) 30cm³   b) 16cm³
   c) 300mm³ d) 15cm³   (1 mark)

2 What is the volume of this prism?
   a) 64cm³   b) 240cm³
   c) 120cm³ d) 20cm³   (1 mark)

3 The volume of a cuboid is 20cm³. If its height is 1cm and its width is 4cm, what is its length?
   a) 5cm   b) 10cm   c) 15cm   d) 8cm   (1 mark)

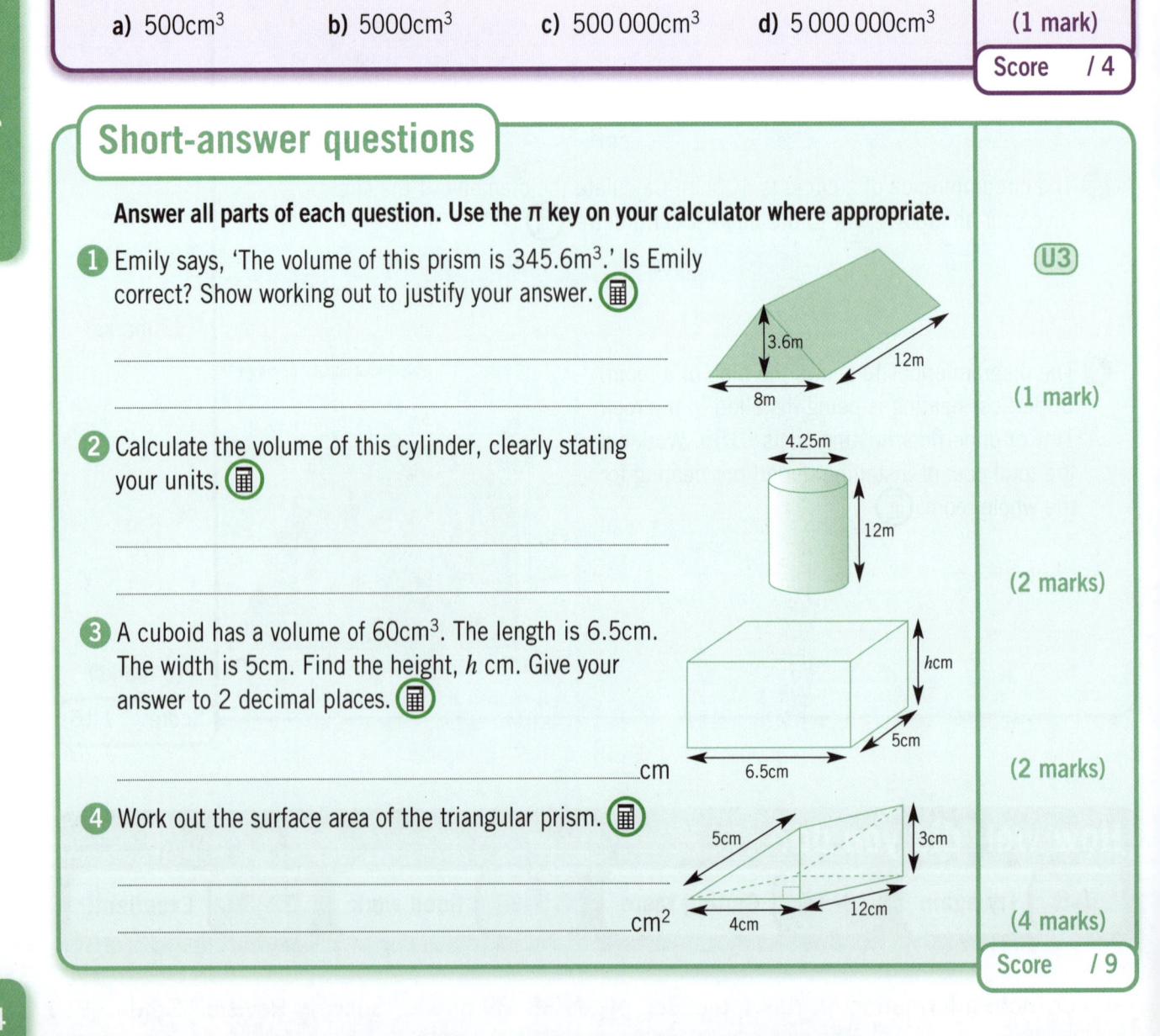

4 What is 5m³ in cm³?
   a) 500cm³   b) 5000cm³   c) 500 000cm³   d) 5 000 000cm³   (1 mark)

Score / 4

Short-answer questions

Answer all parts of each question. Use the π key on your calculator where appropriate.

1 Emily says, 'The volume of this prism is 345.6m³.' Is Emily correct? Show working out to justify your answer.

_____

_____   (1 mark)

2 Calculate the volume of this cylinder, clearly stating your units.

_____

_____   (2 marks)

3 A cuboid has a volume of 60cm³. The length is 6.5cm. The width is 5cm. Find the height, h cm. Give your answer to 2 decimal places.

_____ cm   (2 marks)

4 Work out the surface area of the triangular prism.

_____ cm²   (4 marks)

Score / 9

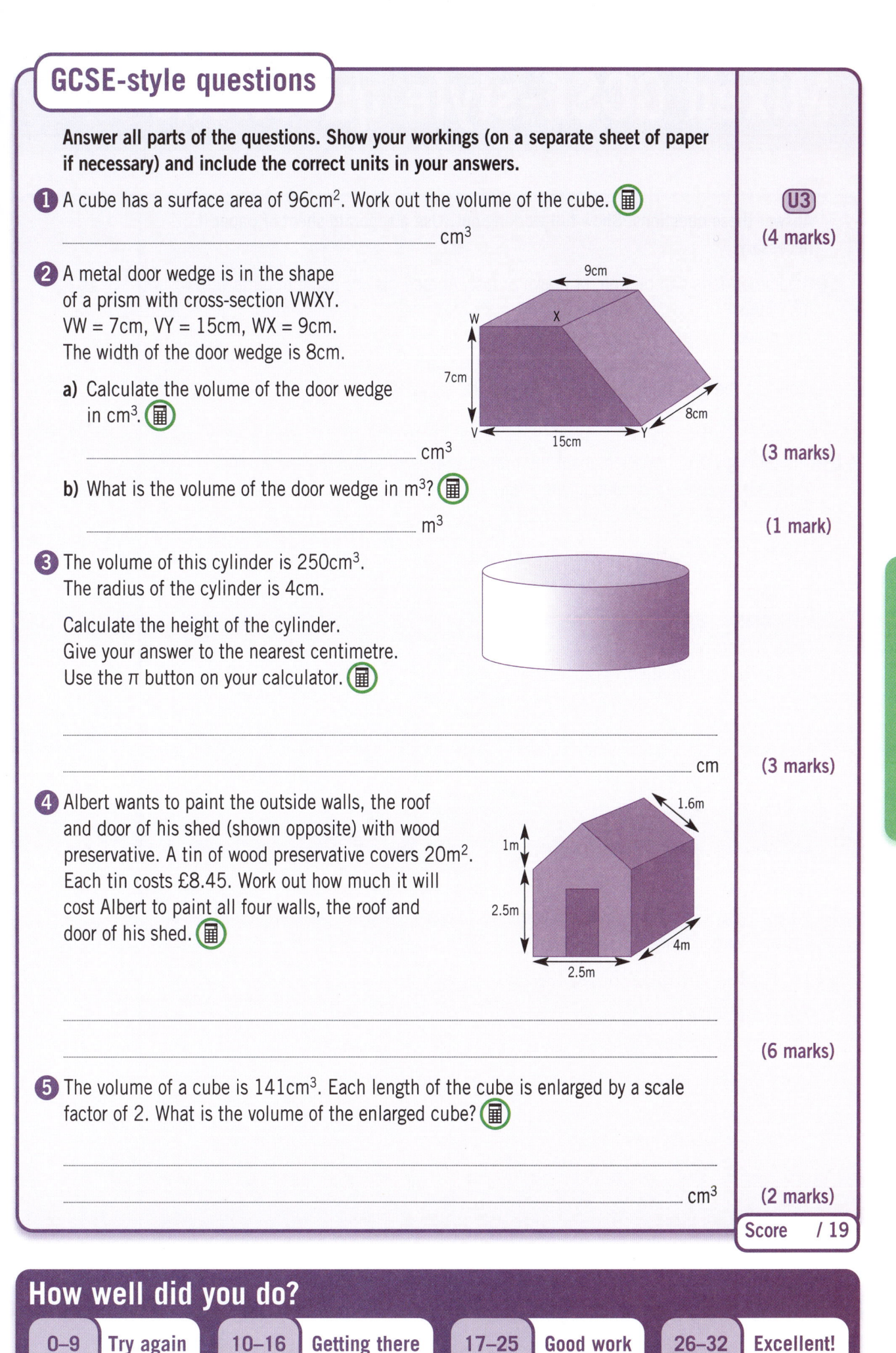

GCSE-style questions

Answer all parts of the questions. Show your workings (on a separate sheet of paper if necessary) and include the correct units in your answers.

1 A cube has a surface area of 96cm². Work out the volume of the cube.

_____ cm³

(U3)
(4 marks)

2 A metal door wedge is in the shape of a prism with cross-section VWXY. VW = 7cm, VY = 15cm, WX = 9cm. The width of the door wedge is 8cm.

a) Calculate the volume of the door wedge in cm³.

_____ cm³

(3 marks)

b) What is the volume of the door wedge in m³?

_____ m³

(1 mark)

3 The volume of this cylinder is 250cm³. The radius of the cylinder is 4cm.

Calculate the height of the cylinder. Give your answer to the nearest centimetre. Use the π button on your calculator.

_____ cm

(3 marks)

4 Albert wants to paint the outside walls, the roof and door of his shed (shown opposite) with wood preservative. A tin of wood preservative covers 20m². Each tin costs £8.45. Work out how much it will cost Albert to paint all four walls, the roof and door of his shed.

(6 marks)

5 The volume of a cube is 141cm³. Each length of the cube is enlarged by a scale factor of 2. What is the volume of the enlarged cube?

_____ cm³

(2 marks)

Score / 19

How well did you do?

| 0–9 Try again | 10–16 Getting there | 17–25 Good work | 26–32 Excellent! |

For more information on this topic, see pages 90–91 of your Success Revision Guide.

Mixed GCSE-style questions

Answer these questions. Show full working out. Use a separate sheet of paper if necessary.

1 A game of darts can be won, or drawn or lost. Ahmed plays a game of darts with his friend.
The probability that Ahmed wins the game is 0.25
The probability that Ahmed draws the game is 0.35
Work out the probability that Ahmed loses the game of darts.

(2 marks)

2 The table gives information about the brands of television available in a shop.

Brand of television	Number in stock
Sharp	6
Panasonic	10
Toshiba	2

Draw an accurate pie chart to show this information.

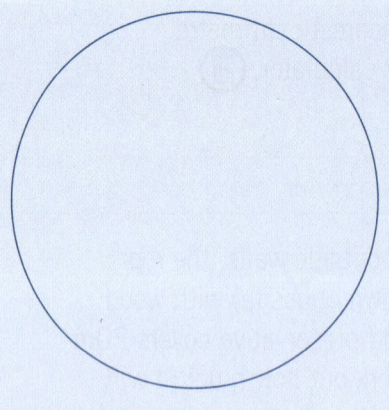

(3 marks)

3 10 boys and 10 girls are given 20 spellings to learn. Here are the correct number of answers for each girl.

14, 15, 13, 14, 10, 12, 8, 18, 19, 11

The range of the boys' scores is 11.
The mean of the boys' scores is 14.

Use the data to investigate the hypothesis: girls are better at spelling than boys.

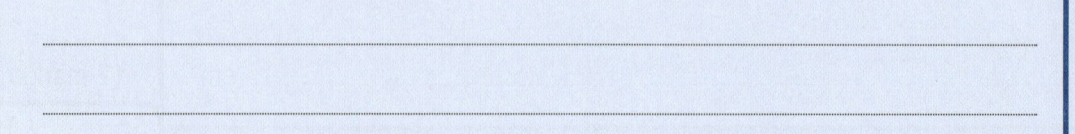

(3 marks)

4. The table gives the times, to the nearest minute, taken to complete a puzzle.

Time (nearest minute)	Frequency
$0 \leq t < 10$	5
$10 \leq t < 20$	12
$20 \leq t < 30$	8
$30 \leq t < 40$	5

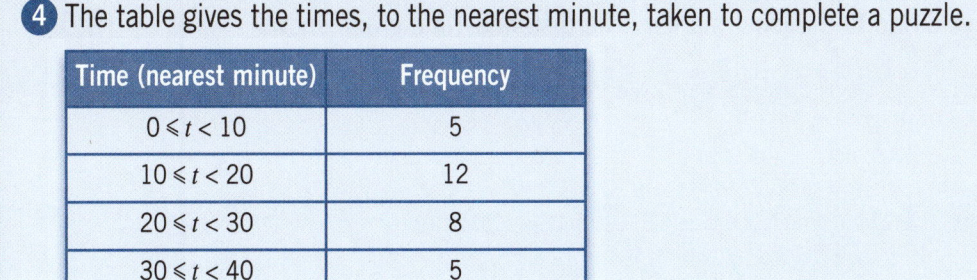

Calculate an estimate for the mean number of minutes taken to complete the puzzle.

Mean = _____ minutes

(4 marks)

5. The two frequency polygons show the heights of a group of year 7 girls and boys.

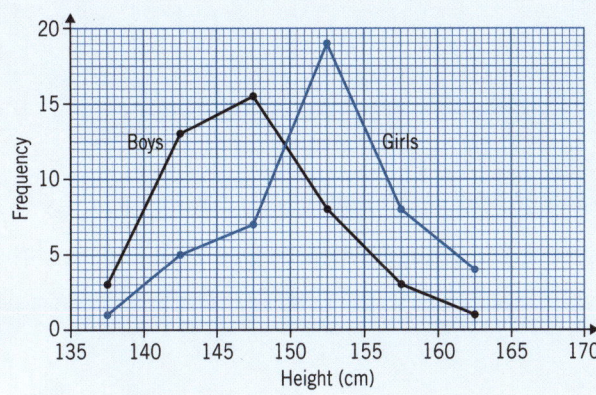

Compare the heights of the boys and girls. Give a reason for your answer.

_____

_____

(3 marks)

6. Write the ratio 32 : 8 in its simplest form.

_____

(1 mark)

7. Katy sells CDs. She sells each CD for £9.20 plus VAT at 17.5%. She sells 127 CDs. Work out how much money Katy receives.

£ _____

(4 marks)

8. a) A water meter at a house records the volume of water used, in cubic metres. During a three-month period, the cost of water at a house is £84. The sewage charge is 95% of the cost of the water. Find the sewage charge.

£ _____

(2 marks)

b) A school uses 17 cubic metres of water one week and 22 cubic metres in the following week. Calculate the percentage increase in the consumption of water.

_____ %

(3 marks)

9 William went for a cycle ride to the local market. The distance–time graph shows his ride.

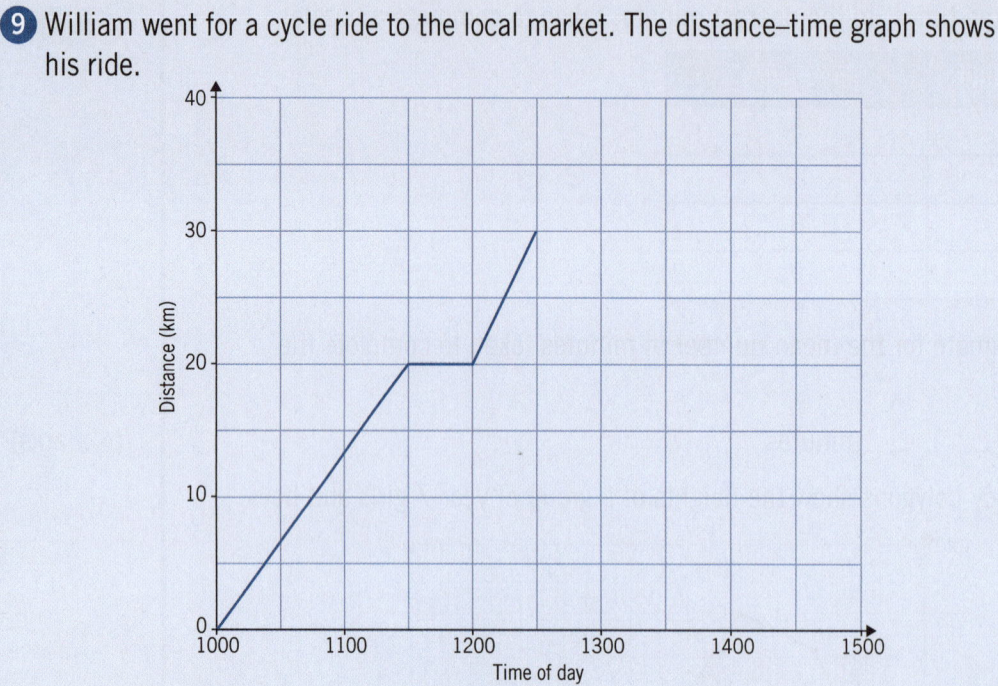

He set off from home at 1000 and arrived at the market at 1230.

a) Explain what might have happened to William when he was 20 kilometres from home.

....

.... (1 mark)

b) At what speed did William travel in the first 20 kilometres?

.... (2 marks)

William stayed at the market for 30 minutes and then cycled home at 25 kilometres per hour.

c) Complete the distance–time graph to show this information. (3 marks)

d) At approximately what time did William arrive home? .... (1 mark)

10 The cost of eight pencils is £1.92. Work out the cost of 14 pencils.

£ .... (2 marks)

11 The table below shows the cost of a double room at a hotel.

| | Cost per person per night ||
Day	Friday to Sunday	Monday to Thursday
Low season	£40.00	£52.00
High season	£45.00	£60.00
Peak season	£60.00	£75.00

Breakfast at the hotel costs £10.50 per person. Mr and Mrs Brown stay in a double room for two nights in peak season. They arrive on Sunday and leave on Tuesday morning. They eat breakfast on Monday morning only. How much does it cost Mr and Mrs Brown to stay at the hotel?

£ .... (3 marks)

12 Comics cost £2.10 each. Calvin buys four comics. He pays with a £20 note. How much change will he get?

(3 marks)

13 Here is a list of eight numbers. 2, 7, 15, 18, 27, 39, 45, 46

   a) Write down two numbers from the list with a sum of 63.

(1 mark)

   b) Write down a number from the list that is a factor of 21.

(1 mark)

   c) Write down a number from the list that is a cube number.

(1 mark)

   d) Write down a number from the list that is a multiple of 5.

(1 mark)

14 Work out 279 × 48

(3 marks)

15 Here are the first four terms of an arithmetic sequence: 5, 9, 13, 17
Find an expression, in terms of n, for the nth term of the sequence.

(2 marks)

16 The diagram shows the positions of three towns, A, B and C. Town C is due east of towns A and B. Town B is due east of A.

A   B   C

Town B is $3\frac{1}{3}$ miles from town A. Town C is $1\frac{1}{4}$ miles from town B.
Calculate the number of miles between town A and town C.

_____ miles (3 marks)

17 Draw the graph of $y = 4 - 3x$ on the grid below.

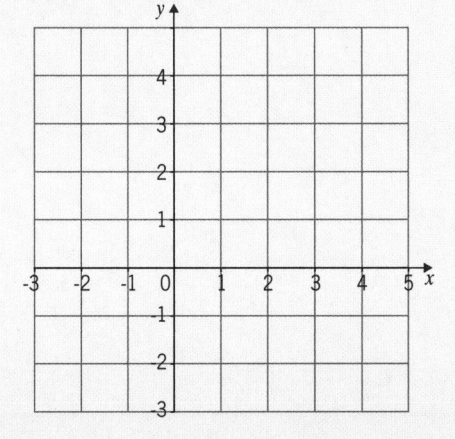

(3 marks)

18 The nth term of a sequence is given by $2n - 3$. Charlotte says that the fifth term of the sequence is 22. Explain whether Charlotte is correct.

(2 marks)

19 Below is a payment plan for Lynette's mobile phone. She receives a bill every month.

Payment Plan
£7 per month
plus
4p per minute

a) In March, Lynette did not make any calls. How much was her bill?

£.. (1 mark)

b) In April, Lynette made 79 minutes of calls. How much was her bill?

£.. (2 marks)

c) In May, Lynette's bill was £9.20. How many minutes of calls did she make?

.... minutes (2 marks)

20 Simplify the following:

a) $p^4 \times p^6$ .... (1 mark)

b) $\dfrac{p^7}{p^3}$ .... (1 mark)

c) $\dfrac{p^4 \times p^5}{p}$ .... (1 mark)

21 a) Simplify $3a + 5b + 2a - 4b$

.... (2 marks)

b) Simplify $7x - 2y + 3x - 5y$

.... (2 marks)

c) Simplify $5a^2 - 3a^2$

.... (1 mark)

22 a) Solve $5n + 2 = 12$

$n = $ .... (2 marks)

b) Solve $4a + 3 = 2a + 8$

$a = $ .... (2 marks)

c) Solve $5x - 2 = 3(x + 6)$

$x = $ .... (2 marks)

d) Solve $\dfrac{3 - 2x}{4} = 2$

$x = $ .... (2 marks)

23 Look at the shaded shape on the centimetre grid.

   a) i) Find the area of the shaded shape.

   _____ cm² (1 mark)

   ii) Find the perimeter of the shaded shape.

   _____ cm (1 mark)

   b) The diagram shows a square.
   Draw the lines of symmetry on the square.

   (2 marks)

24 The shape of a disused fish pond is a cylinder as shown. 1m³ of soil weighs 1.25 tonnes. A gardener wants to fill the pond with soil as cheaply as possible. The table shows the cost that two companies charge to do this.

Gardener's Soil	£52 per tonne	Delivery £25
Tops' Soil	7 tonnes for £340, then £68.25 per extra tonne	Free delivery

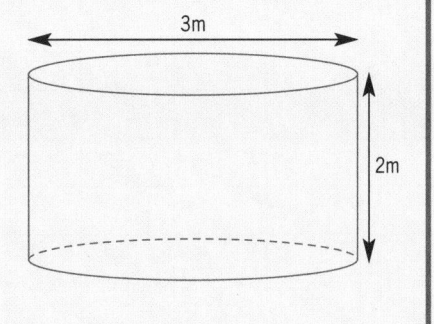

Which company should the gardener use and how much will it cost?

(6 marks)

25 In the diagram, WXY is a straight line.

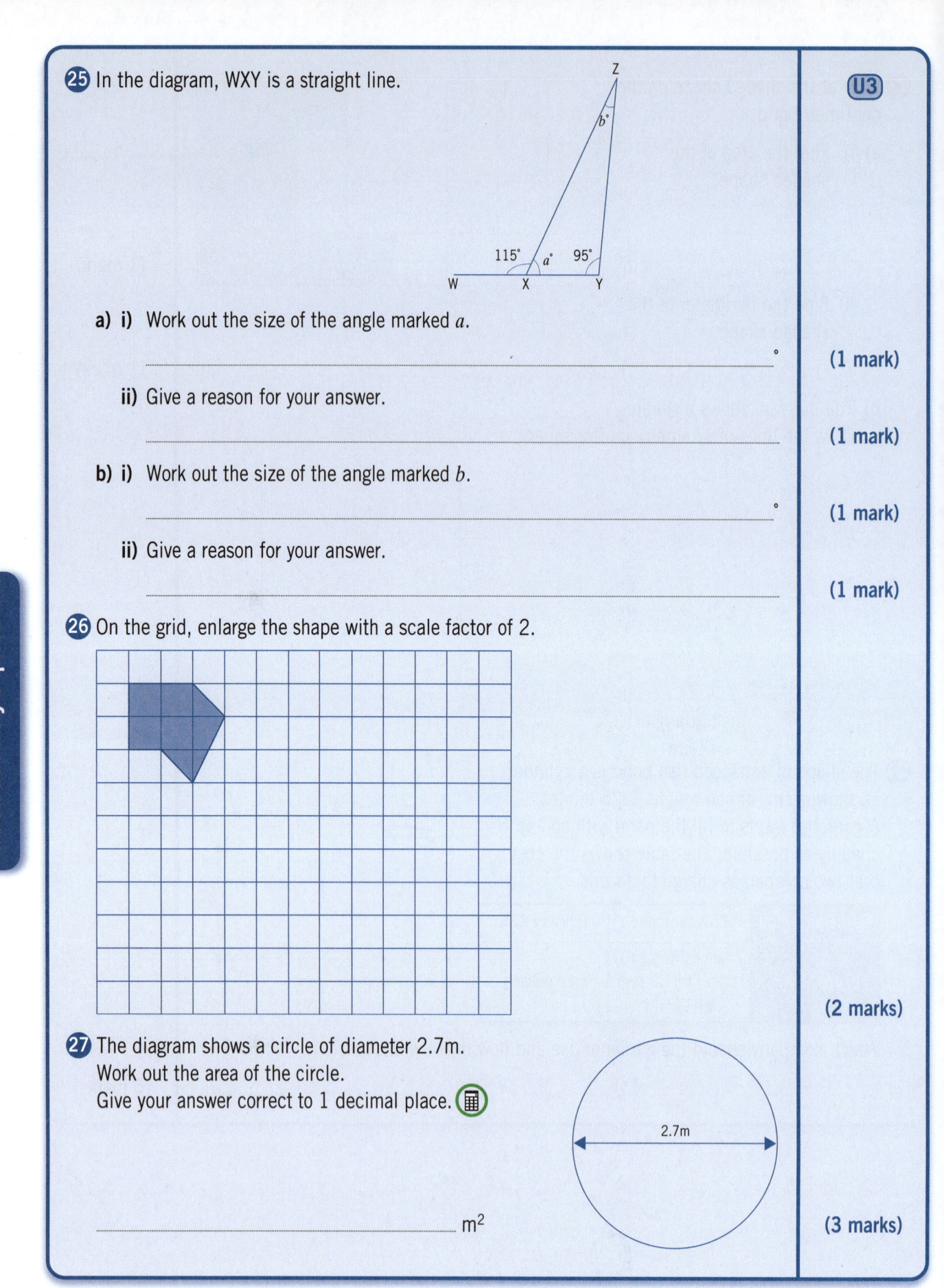

a) i) Work out the size of the angle marked *a*.

   _____° (1 mark)

   ii) Give a reason for your answer.

   _____ (1 mark)

b) i) Work out the size of the angle marked *b*.

   _____° (1 mark)

   ii) Give a reason for your answer.

   _____ (1 mark)

26 On the grid, enlarge the shape with a scale factor of 2.

(2 marks)

27 The diagram shows a circle of diameter 2.7m.
Work out the area of the circle.
Give your answer correct to 1 decimal place.

_____ m² (3 marks)

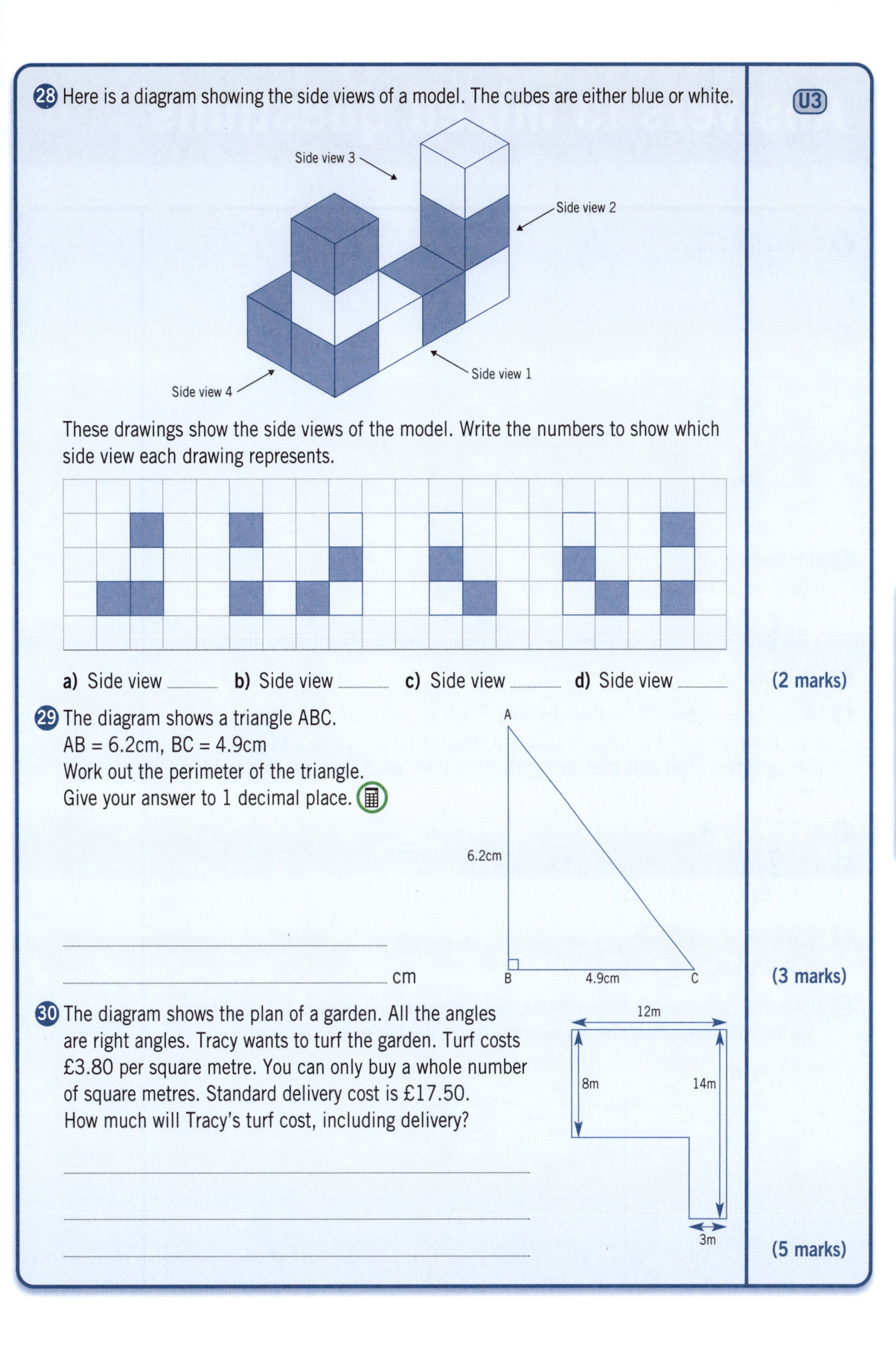

28) Here is a diagram showing the side views of a model. The cubes are either blue or white.

These drawings show the side views of the model. Write the numbers to show which side view each drawing represents.

a) Side view _____ b) Side view _____ c) Side view _____ d) Side view _____ (2 marks)

29) The diagram shows a triangle ABC.
AB = 6.2cm, BC = 4.9cm
Work out the perimeter of the triangle.
Give your answer to 1 decimal place.

_____ cm   (3 marks)

30) The diagram shows the plan of a garden. All the angles are right angles. Tracy wants to turf the garden. Turf costs £3.80 per square metre. You can only buy a whole number of square metres. Standard delivery cost is £17.50. How much will Tracy's turf cost, including delivery?

(5 marks)

Answers to mixed questions

1) 1 − (0.25 + 0.35)
= 1 − 0.6
= 0.4

2)

Sharp 120°, Toshiba 40°, Panasonic 200°

3) Girls range = 11
Girls mean score = 13.4
Conclusion: boys are better at spelling than girls as their mean is higher and their range is the same **or** there is no difference as the means and ranges are about the same.

4) 19.$\dot{3}$ minutes

5) The girls are generally taller than the boys. There are more tall girls than tall boys, since there are 4 girls in the 160–165cm class interval compared with 1 boy. There are more short boys than short girls since there are 3 boys and only 1 girl in the 135–140cm class interval.

6) 4 : 1

7) 9.20 × 1.175 = £10.81 with VAT for each CD
127 × £10.81 = £1372.87

8) a) 0.95 × £84 = £79.80

b) $\frac{5}{17}$ × 100% = 29.4% (1 d.p.)

9) a) He may have decided to have a rest, met somebody and stopped to talk or had a flat tyre. (Any reasonable explanation, which implies that he stopped.)

b) 13.$\dot{3}$ km/h

c)

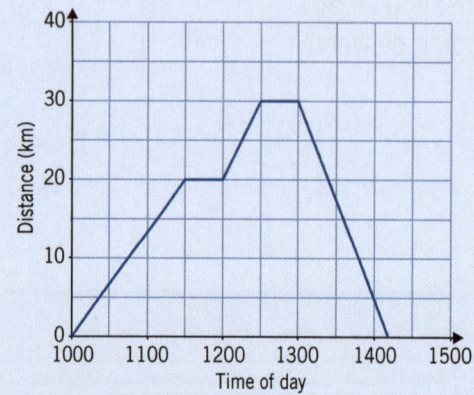

d) Approximately between 1410 and 1415.

10 £3.36

11 Sunday night: 2 × £60.00 = £120.00
Monday night: 2 × £75.00 = £150.00
Breakfast: 2 × £10.50 = £21.00
Total cost = £291.00

12 4 × £2.10 = £8.40
£20 − £8.40 = £11.60

13 a) 45 and 18   **b)** 7   **c)** 27   **d)** 15 or 45

14 13 392

15 $4n + 1$

16 $4\frac{7}{12}$ miles

17

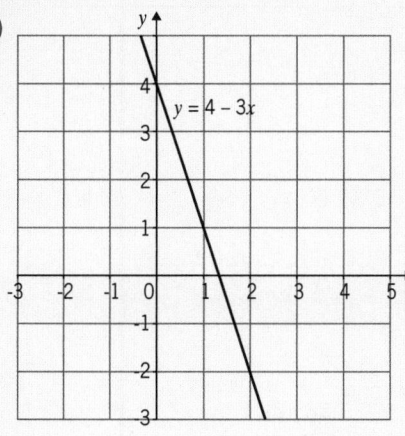

18 If $n = 5$, $2n − 3 = 2 × 5 − 3 = 7$. Charlotte is not correct.

19 a) £7   **b)** £7 + (79 × 0.04) = £10.16   **c)** 55 minutes

20 a) p^{10} **b)** p^4 **c)** p^8

21 a) $5a + b$ **b)** $10x − 7y$ **c)** $2a^2$

22 a) $5n + 2 = 12$
      $5n = 12 − 2$
      $5n = 10$
      $n = 2$

  b) $4a + 3 = 2a + 8$
      $2a = 5$
      $a = 2.5$

  c) $x = 10$

  d) $x = -2.5$

23 a) i) 11cm²   **ii)** 18cm

  b)

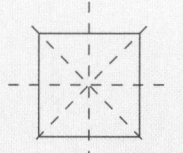

24 Volume = π × r² × h
= π × 1.5² × 2
= 14.137...m³

Soil needed = 14.137 × 1.25
= 17.67 tonnes
hence 18 tonnes are needed

Gardeners' Soil: 18 × £52 + £25 = £961
Tops' Soil: £340 + 11 × £68.25 = £1090.75

Gardeners' Soil is the cheapest.

25 a) i) 65° **ii)** Angles on a straight line add up to 180°
  b) i) 20° **ii)** Angles in a triangle add up to 180° (95° + 65° + 20° = 180°)

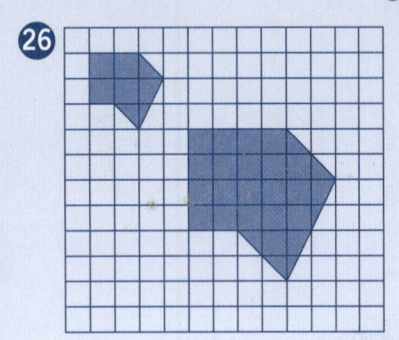

26

27 Area = π × r²   r = $\frac{2.7}{2}$ r = 1.35
Area = π × 1.35²
= 5.725
= 5.7m²

28 a) Side view 4 **b)** Side view 1 **c)** Side view 2 **d)** Side view 3

29 Let AC = x
x² = 6.2² + 4.9²
x² = 38.44 + 24.01
x² = 62.45
x = √62.45
x = 7.9cm (1 d.p.)
Perimeter = 6.2 + 4.9 + 7.9
= 19cm

30 Area of garden: (12 × 8) + (6 × 3)
= 96 + 18
= 114m²
Cost of turf: 114 × £3.80
= £433.20 + £17.50 delivery = £450.70